The *Surprising* Mr Kipling

An anthology and re-assessment of the poetry of Rudyard Kipling

BRIAN HARRIS

The **Surprising** Mr Kipling
Copyright © 2013 Brian Harris
Second, corrected impression 2014.

ISBN: 1494221942
ISBN 13: 9781494221942

Cover design incorporates a sketch by Sarah Harris.

For

Tom Harris, Tom Roffey, Ernest Roffey

and Herbert Hodgson.

Four 'Old Contemptibles'

CONTENTS

In awarding Kipling the Nobel Prize for Literature the Nobel Prize Committee cited a passage from one of his poems as, 'reveal[ing] that yearning for a patiently sought, never to be attained ideal that resides in living form in the breast of every true poet.' The passage read:

> Thy face is far from this our war,
> Our call and counter-cry,
> I shall not find Thee quick and kind,
> Nor know Thee till I die,
> Enough for me in dreams to see
> And touch Thy garments' hem:
> Thy feet have trod so near to God
> I may not follow them.[1]

---

1 *To the True Romance.*

FOREWORD

By Dr. Lizzy Welby

> If I have given you delight
> By aught that I have done
> Let me lie quiet in that night
> Which shall be yours anon

The lines that open Kipling's *'The Appeal'* read as an entreaty by an author so fiercely protective of his privacy during his lifetime that he destroyed vast piles of personal papers and correspondence. Biographers Charles Carrington and Lord Birkenhead provide insights into much material that has since been lost, due to Kipling's daughter Elsie Bambridge continuing the obliteration of her father's papers. Kipling hated biographies. He referred to the practice as 'higher cannibalism' and disliked the idea of his private life laid bare for a public hungry to devour. He didn't have much time for the Kipling Society either: it was for his output as a writer that he wanted to be remembered. And what an output. It is difficult even to pin him down to a genre. Arguably, one of the best short story writers that Britain has seen, he was also a dab hand at parodies and sketches, verse and fiction. He wrote novels, travelogues, speeches and inscriptions. He could write for children and adults; imbue his fiction with authentic voices, be they those of children or adults, animals or machines.

He was a reluctant award-winner, quietly down-playing the accolades heaped upon him by a pre-war public hungry for his precocious talent.

In 1907, he won the Nobel Prize for Literature at the age of only forty-two and the Gold Medal of the Royal Society of Literature in 1926 – an honour only shared with Scott, Meredith and Hardy before him. Yet an appreciation of his art continues to be marred by the politics attached to the man. After the horror of the First World War, a wider public revolted against a writer seen as having been responsible for a generation of their young men imaging Armageddon as a 'lark', eager to give the 'Hun' a good bashing. It seemed as though Kipling would be consigned to history as, to borrow from John Osborne, 'just one of those sturdy old plants left over from the Edwardian Wilderness who can't understand why the sun isn't shining anymore'.[2]

Kipling's art, however, refuses to sink below the waves of contemporary tastes. Much has been done in recent decades to unshackle Kipling's legacy as spokesperson for the monolithic edifice of empire. Increasingly, the complexities of his verse and fiction are being scrutinised under a post-colonial critical microscope. Modern biographer David Gilmour's study of Kipling's imperial and political life is a thoughtful examination of Kipling's many identities,[3] particularly when read in conjunction with Harry Ricketts' biography, where he aims to 'bring out- the full range of these diverse Kiplings'.[4] From Edmund Wilson (1941)[5] to Andrew Rutherford (1964)[6] much has been done to wrest Kipling from his hard-line imperial propagandist image, delivering tired aphorisms and revelling in revenge.[7] Wilson in particular was important in initiating

---

2 John Osborne, *Look Back in Anger* (London: Penguin, 1982), p. 66.

3 David Gilmour, *The Long Recessional: The Imperial Life of Rudyard Kipling* (London: John Murray, 2002). Carrington, Birkenhead, Gilmour and Ricketts will be the main sources for details of Kipling's life but these will be supplemented by additional references to Andrew Lycett's lengthy and in-depth historical study *Rudyard Kipling* (London: Phoenix, 2000)

4 Harry Ricketts, *The Unforgiving Minute: A Life of Rudyard Kipling* (London: Chatto & Windus, 1999), p. xi.

5 Edmund Wilson, 'The Kipling that Nobody Read', in *Kipling's Mind and Art*, ed. by Andrew Rutherford (Stanford: Stanford University Press, 1964), pp. 17-69.

6 Andrew Rutherford, 'Officers and Gentlemen', in *Kipling's Mind and Art*, pp. 171-198.

7 However, cruelty and revenge are recurring themes in Kipling's fiction.

what Martin Seymour-Smith calls a 'sensible criticism of Kipling'.[8] J.M.S. Tompkins argues that 'no one should pass judgement on the "tone" of a writer more than one generation away from him'[9] and now we see Kipling being appraised more sympathetically[10] by critics who are responding to his art through the distancing effects of time.[11]

Kipling always wanted to be remembered for his words: 'And for the little, little, span /The dead are borne in mind, / Seek not to question other than /The books I leave behind.' As the seemingly eternal British Empire was dashed on the altar of time, so Kipling's art is slowly being released from its ironclad ideological fist. I think he would have been quietly and reverently pleased that his words have outlasted his political legacy.

---

8 Martin Seymour-Smith, *Rudyard Kipling* (London: Macdonald, Queen Anne Press, 1989), p. 6.

9 *The Art of Rudyard Kipling*, p. xi.

10 For example, C. S. Lewis, *Selected Literary Essays*, ed. by Walter Hooper (Cambridge: Cambridge University Press, 1969) and *A Choice of Kipling's* Verse, with Eliot's caveat that Kipling's artistic dexterity was largely accidental, and Kingsley Amis, *Rudyard Kipling and His World*.

11 As captured in Auden's 'In Memory of W. B. Yeats', 'Time with this strange excuse/Pardoned Kipling and his views,/And will pardon Paul Claudel,/Pardons him for writing well.' *W. H. Auden Selected Poems*, ed. by John Fuller (London: Faber & Faber, 2005), p. 35.

PREFACE

It was during a long hot Summer childhood that I chanced upon Rudyard Kipling's short stories on the bookshelves of a family friend's house in the country, and immersed myself in them with joy. It was not until much later that I discovered his poetry and began to wonder why so little of it was well known.

Throughout Kipling's career - and since - praise and disparagement have been his lot in almost equal measure. Today he is acknowledged as one of our finest short story writers and the author of at least one truly great novel, but his poetry has not yet received the recognition it deserves. Which is odd because, three quarters of a century after his death, many of his poems are still household names, and their phrases litter our speech. So why do we need another anthology of his verse?

Even while Kipling was being scorned by the critics framed copies of his poem, 'If-' hung, like icons, on countless bedroom walls. Beyond that, however, he was known mainly for his children's verse and for a handful of over-anthologized 'treasures'. Familiarity, it seems, had dulled the effect of his most well known pieces, while many equally fine poems were neglected. What is lacking, therefore is, not another selection of Kipling's 'best' work, but one which demonstrates the extraordinary width and depth of his talents and the light which they throw on this great but enigmatic author.

And that is what this book aims to provide.

To this end such excellent but time-worn pieces as 'Gunga Din', 'The White Man's Burden', 'Danny Deever' and 'The Way Through the Woods', have been replaced in this anthology by equally important, but less well known works, such as 'Heriot's Ford', 'Lichtenberg', 'A Singer Speaks to a Wayside Well' and 'A Dawn Wind', as well as minor gems like 'My Rival', 'A Song of Tommy' and 'The Prodigal Son'. For every 'Mandalay' I have substituted a 'Bridge-guard at the Karoo'; for every 'Smuggler's Song', a 'Looking Glass'; and for every 'Recessional', an 'American Rebellion'. Instead of the justly celebrated 'McAndrew's Hymn' I offer what to me is its more thoughtful sister piece, 'Mary Gloster'. Finally, with the first centenary of the Great War fast approaching I am pleased to include most of Kipling's brilliant, Epitaphs of the War.

This is a risky strategy which has not been tried before, but I believe it to be one that, if judged correctly, could prompt a fresh appraisal of Kipling the poet and introduce readers to the delights of a much wider range of his verse.

I am not a poet, an academic or a critic, merely an unashamed enthusiast of Kipling's verse. Whatever success this book may enjoy will depend in part on how well I have succeeded in passing that passion on to the reader, but above all on the merits of the verse itself.

BH

January, 2014

ACKNOWLEDGEMENTS

This anthology could not have been produced without the many biographers and critics of Rudyard Kipling on whose work I have drawn heavily. For anyone coming fresh to the subject I would recommend as a first biography Andrew Lycett's *Rudyard Kipling*. For critical background, I would go to Roger Lancelyn Green's *Kipling The Critical Heritage* (now in urgent need of updating). For guidance on the poetry I suggest Prof. Dobrée's *Rudyard Kipling, Realist and Fabulist* (though there is need for many more such studies).

I have been fortunate to be preparing this book at a time when Prof. Pinney's splendid *Cambridge Edition of the Poems of Rudyard Kipling* has just been published, and have relied on his text throughout. Except where otherwise indicated, a reference to an authority in this book (Pinney, Lycett etc) denotes the relevant work noted in the Select Bibliography at the end of this book.

It is well known that Kipling had little time for the Society that bears his name, but as a relatively new member of that illustrious body I have been impressed by the learning and comprehensiveness of its web site, in particular the New Readers' Guide, which I cannot praise too highly. I am also grateful to those members who suggested poems which I had overlooked.

I am obliged to Dr Lizzy Welby for providing a Foreword to help launch this book upon an unsuspecting world and to the Society's librarian, John Walker for reading the manuscript. His encyclopaedic knowledge of the author and all his works has helped me avoid many pitfalls; and his wise and perceptive suggestions have improved the content immeasurably.

Responsibility for any remaining errors and defects rests, of course, upon no one other than myself.

B.H.

A BRIEF LIFE
OF RUDYARD KIPLING

Rudyard Kipling was born in Bombay[12] on the west coast of India on 30 December 1865[13]. Decades later he recalled it as the 'Mother of Cities to me,/For I was born in her gate,/Between the palms and the sea,/Where the world-end steamers wait.'[14]

Rudyard's parents lived in a house in the grounds of the Jeejeebhoy School of Art and Industry, of which his father was Principal and professor of architectural sculpture. His mother, the lively and gifted Alice, came from the talented Macdonald family. One of her sisters married Sir Edward Burne-Jones, the painter; another married a future president of the Royal Academy, while yet a third was the mother of Stanley Baldwin, the future Prime Minister. It sounds impressive, but in truth the Macdonalds, like the Kiplings, though people of talent and character, were little better connected than many another middle class couple.

'Ruddy', as he was known in the family, was the Kiplings' first child. The world he was born into was unrecognizable to anyone who had not left England's shores. Brought up by his ayah, or nursemaid, he was familiar with the vernacular before he began to speak English. In old age he recorded how his,

---

12 Now in India called Mumbai.

13 His first name was Joseph. Like his father, John Lockwood Kipling, he elected to use his second name.

14 *To the City of Bombay.*

... first impression [was] of daybreak, light and colour and golden and purple fruits at the level of my shoulder. This would be the memory of early morning walks to the Bombay fruit market with my ayah and later with my sister in her perambulator, and of our returns with our purchases piled high on the bows of it ... I have always felt the menacing darkness of tropical eventides, as I have loved the voices of night-winds through palm or banana leaves, and the song of the tree-frogs.[15]

He never lost the feeling of a mysterious sub-continent, where,
A stone's throw out on either hand
From that well-ordered road we tread,
And all the world is wild and strange;
Churel and ghoul and Djinn and sprite.[16]

Ruddy had been born after an arduous six day confinement and his mother decided to have her next child in England. When she came she was christened Alice after her mother, but came to be known in the family as Trix. After the loss of a third child Alice resolved that Ruddy and Trix should be brought up in England. It was an arrangement common among Anglo-Indian[17] parents, but, instead of leaving the children with any one of their many loving relatives, Alice elected to send them to foster parents chosen from a newspaper advertisement. The only explanation she would give for this unusual arrangement was that, to have done otherwise, would 'have led to complications'. In what was no doubt a well intentioned move, she put the children to bed in their new home and vanished the next morning without a word of explanation. It was not a wise decision. Trix later wrote that 'the real tragedy of our early days ... sprang from our inability to understand why our parents had deserted us.'

---

15 This and other of Kipling's recollections in this chapter come from his autobiographical musings, *Something of Myself*. It is an incomplete record which leaves out more than it contains; much of the poet's internal life remains a mystery.

16 Epigraph to *In the House of Suddhoo* in *Plain Tales from the Hills*.

17 In those days the term, 'Anglo-Indian' meant English people living in India and not, as now, people of mixed parentage.

Ruddy's new home was with the Holloway family in a terrace house with the doleful name of 'Lorne Lodge' in Southsea, then a small town to the east of Portsmouth. The head of the household was an old sea captain who had been a Midshipman at the battle of Navarino. The five year old Ruddy enjoyed their walks together round the dockyards listening to his tales of the sea, but at home the child's life was made miserable by the captain's deeply religious wife. Nearing the end of his life, Kipling recalled his foster home as, 'an establishment run with the full vigour of the Evangelical as revealed to the Woman'. In this she was ably assisted by her bullying son - 'the Devil boy' as Kipling was to call him. The three year old Trix was not immune from the harsh regime - she was made to stand on a table in punishment for her 'crimes'. But, according to Kipling, 'the Woman' reserved her worst 'punishments and humiliation - above all humiliation' - for himself. 'I had never heard of Hell', he wrote, 'so I was introduced to it in all its terrors.... Myself I was regularly beaten.' Such an upbringing would have been difficult for anyone, but for someone who until then had been indulged by loving parents and worshipped by an adoring ayah, Ruddy's six years in Southsea were among the worst of his life.

Kipling's only respite from Lorne Lodge was the 'paradisal' month or so he spent every Christmas at 'The Grange' in Fulham with his beloved Aunt Georgie Burne-Jones and Uncle Ned, the painter; but when that came to an end he had to return to Lorne Lodge. As soon as he learned to read, Kipling found consolation in books, which he consumed voraciously. Whether because of this or otherwise, his eyesight got so bad that he was unable to read beyond the second line on an optician's chart.

Kipling did not do well at the 'terrible little day-school' to which he was sent. For throwing away a bad school report he was 'well beaten and sent to school through the streets of Southsea with the placard "Liar" between my shoulders.' He described how,

> 'Some sort of nervous breakdown followed, for I imagined I
> saw shadows and things that were not there, and they worried me more than the Woman. The beloved Aunt must have
> heard of it, and a man came down to see me as to my eyes and

reported that I was half-blind. This, too, was supposed to be 'showing-off,' and I was segregated from my sister - another punishment - as a sort of moral leper. Then - I do not remember that I had any warning - the Mother returned from India. She told me afterwards that when she first came up to my room to kiss me goodnight, I flung up an arm to guard off the cuff that I had been trained to expect.

As soon as she got to hear of Ruddy's unhappiness, his mother removed him to lodgings in London where he was given the run of the nearby South Kensington Museum (now the Victoria and Albert) an experience which he described as 'a soaking in colour and design'.

Some have suggested that Kipling's recollections of his hardships at Southsea were over-egged, pointing to the fact that, while removing Ruddy from Lorne Lodge, Alice was content to leave his sister, Trix there. It must be conceded that Ruddy was not a model Victorian child. Ricketts describes how, at the age of three while his mother was staying with her parents, he would walk down the street, shouting 'Ruddy is coming!' or, if anyone got in his way, 'An angry Ruddy is coming!' When he finally left, Alice's mother wrote, 'Ruddy's screaming tempers made Papa so ill we were thankful to see them on their way.'

Prof. Pinney concluded: 'There is no evidence that Mrs Holloway was anything but conscientious in the discharge of her stated duty to the children; unluckily, she and the young Rudyard were spiritual opposites, and for him these years were an almost unremitting experience of hell.' It is unlikely that we will ever know the full truth about Southsea.

Some have speculated that Southsea was responsible for the flashes of cruelty and revenge which occasionally appear in the author's works. His short story, *Baa, Baa, Black Sheep*, which is a thinly disguised account of that time, ends with the narrator's comment, '... when young lips have drunk deep of the waters of Hate, Suspicion and Despair, all the Love in the world will not wholly take away that knowledge.' Many years later he seemed to contradict himself when he wrote, 'these things

4

[ie Southsea], and many more of the like, drained me of any capacity for real, personal hate for the rest of my days.' Which simply goes to show how difficult it is to impute motivation to anyone on the basis of childhood experience.

At the age of thirteen, Ruddy was enrolled in the recently founded United Services College at Westward Ho! in Devon. The college, which consisted of 'twelve bleak houses by the shore', had recently been set up by a group of army officers to provide a cheap education for boys intended for Sandhurst. The headmaster, Cormell Price (known as 'Crom') was a Gladstonian Liberal and a friend of Burne-Jones. Kipling came to respect and love him; he was, however, unable to control the bullying that was endemic in his, like so many other, schools of that era. Ruddy, now short, chubby, bespectacled, and with an incipient moustache, was on the sharp end of much of it, until he 'got his strength' at the middle of the second year.

Kipling found relief from the bullying in the friendship and protection of the two boys with whom he shared a study. They were respectively, Lionel Dunsterville, later to become a major-general, and G. C. Beresford, whose career as a civil engineer in India was cut short by malaria. (The sickness proved to be a blessing in disguise because he went on to become a celebrated photographer in England.) Two decades after leaving college, Kipling was to fictionally embellish their juvenile escapades in a collection of stories entitled *Stalky & Co.*, in which Dunsterville became 'Stalky' and Beresford, 'M'Turk', while the author himself appears as 'Beetle'. Many years later he was to pen a mock Ode after the style of the Roman poet, Quintus Horatius Flaccus ('Horace'), which recalled those,

> '... glorious, unforgot-
> ten innocent enormities
> Of frontless days before the beard,
> When, instant on the casual jest,
> The God Himself of Mirth appeared
> And snatched us to His heaving breast ...
> Then He withdrew from sight and speech,

Nor left a shrine. How comes it now,
While Charon's keel grates on the beach,
He calls so clear: 'Rememberest thou?'?[18]

Kipling's education, like Shakespeare's, was neither extensive or exceptional: from the point of view of his future career he probably gained as much from being given the run of Crom's library and the editorship of the school magazine, as from the classroom. It was during these years that he took his first tentative steps into verse, some of which his mother was to publish without consulting him.

The young Kipling was as precocious in his emotional maturity as his physical. At the age of fourteen, while visiting Trix at Lorne Lodge, he met and fell for one of her fellow boarders, a girl of Pre-Raphaelite looks, by the name of Florence (or 'Flo') Garrard (of the famous jewellery family). It was a strong attachment, at least on Kipling's part, which he was to break off only after returning to India.

After he left college Ruddy's parents could not afford to send him to Oxford and judged him insufficiently bright to win a scholarship. (The lost opportunity seems to have rankled with him for a long time.) Fortunately, his father was able to help. Now removed to Lahore in the far North of India, he held the posts of Principal of the Mayo School of Art and curator of the city Museum, and was able to find his son a post as sub-editor to the local English language daily paper, the Civil and Military Gazette (the 'CMG'). Kipling described his return to India thus:

> 'So, at sixteen years and nine months, but looking four or five years older, and adorned with real whiskers which the scandalised Mother abolished within one hour of beholding, I found myself at Bombay where I was born ...'

---

18   *To the companions.* 'Horace, Book V. Ode 17.' See also the poem, *A School Song* (not included.)

From Bombay, Kipling travelled by train a thousand or so miles north to take up his new job. It was to be a hard apprenticeship in the course of which he had to,

> 'edit the day's telegrams from the news-agencies, summarise the latest official reports, skim through some 30 other newspapers of all sorts for stories, sub-edit contributions sent in by readers and others, and deal with social, sporting and other local events, as well as making up the entire copy and reading the proofs in time to go to press at midnight, working never less than 10, and sometimes as much as 16 hours a day, even in the hot season, when the indoor temperature ranged between 85 and something over 100 degrees Fahrenheit.'[19]

The pace was gruelling, but as he wrote,
> ... while each new day brings some new thought
> And life's chain sparkles, golden link by link
> Write quickly; good or evil, all is fraught
> More deeply than you think.[20]

Kipling was fortunate to survive the local climate. He later recollected how,

> [d]eath was always our near companion. When there was an outbreak of eleven cases of typhoid in our white community of seventy, and professional nurses had not been invented, the men sat up with the men and the women with the women. We lost four of our invalids and thought we had done well. Otherwise, men and women dropped where they stood. Hence our custom of looking up any one who did not appear at our daily gatherings.[21]

It nearly led to another breakdown.

---

19 George Engle in the archive of the Kipling Society.
20 *As One Who Throws Earth's Gold Away in Scorn.*
21 *Something of Myself.*

Such time as the young journalist was able to snatch from his labours he chose to spend in the rather grand premises of the Punjab club, where he 'met none except picked men at their definite work—Civilians, Army, Education, Canals, Forestry, Engineering, Irrigation, Railways, Doctors, and Lawyers—samples of each branch and each talking his own shop.' (Fascination with 'shop' was to be a lasting feature of his writings.) He dined in the officers' mess where the sherry was fortified by 30 grains of quinine. Another lasting source of inspiration were his frequent visits to the army barracks at the Mian Mir cantonments (or barracks), where he formed easy friendships among the private soldiers. Charles Allen tells how the young journalist met a Colour Sergeant and, through him, was introduced to '8 or 10 boozing chums' who belonged to the musket fatigue party. It was from yarns like theirs that Kipling obtained much of the inspiration for the stories and poems that were to make his name.

Kipling was horrified and entranced in equal measure by the great city of Lahore. In an engrossing sketch entitled *The City of Dreadful Night* he claimed that he had spent 'one weary night on the great minar[22] of the mosque of Wazir Khan looking down upon the heat tortured city of Lahore and seventy thousand men and women sleeping in the moon light'. Though no slave to opium, his occasional experiments with the drug may have provided a background to some of his weirder tales. He also seems to have enjoyed an active sex life among his Anglo-Indian friends.[23]

Less well known is the poet's brief venture onto the boards. In 1883 he took part in an amateur production, playing the head of the Paris police at the beginning of the nineteenth century. His paper claimed that he displayed 'a talent for acting', though the critic could hardly be said to have been impartial. Kipling commemorated the occasion with an eerie poem addressed to a lady friend entitled, *Max Desmarets His Valentine*. The eponymous corpse, by then long interred in the *Pére La Chaise* cemetery, describes how,

---

22 Minars were tall Mughal milestones.
23 Allen.

Seventy years in a coffin pent
Little of beauty have I to show,
Seventy years will alter one so
With a coffin lid for a firmament
And the inky darkness night and day;
What wonder, then, if I fall away ...
In place of a heart my white ribs shine ...
Pity a skeleton Valentine.

Like many poets Kipling learned his craft by example. Even as a child he had been a talented parodist, aping the writers he most admired, Browning, Fitzgerald, Swinburne, Tennyson and the Roman poet, Horace.[24] But it was only when he began to write about the social life of the British in India that Kipling found a voice of his own. In 1886 he published his first significant collection of poems: *Departmental Ditties*. This small volume consisted mostly of satirical pieces which the historian, Sir William Hunter described as 'reflect[ing] with light gaiety the thoughts and feelings of actual men and women, [that] are true as well as clever'[25]. At the time, however, the book was no more than a modest success and Kipling refused to include any of its contents in his first two collections of verse, judging them 'worthless'. He later relented.[26]

At the age of 22, but looking more like 40, Kipling was posted to a better paid job on the CMG's more prestigeful sister paper, the *Pioneer*. It entailed a move to the city of Allahabad in central India on the banks of the Ganges. As a sort of roving correspondent he had a weekly supplement to fill, which gave him the opportunity to gain yet further experience of the many castes and religions of the great sub-continent.

During the baking hot Summer months Kipling, like many of his fellow countrymen, fled to Simla, a cool hill town in the foothills of the Himalayas, some six hundred miles to the north. How the

24 Their influence could still be seen many years later, as for example in this couplet after the manner of Blake: *'When a Woman kills a Chicken/Dynasties and Empires sicken.' As Easy as ABC*. Family Magazine, January – March, 1912.

25 Essay in *Kipling the Critical Heritage*.

26 Pinney.

Anglo-Indians conducted themselves in this closed environment was the inspiration for his first collection of prose. In 1888 some of the stories he had written for the CMG were collected in book form under the title, *Plain Tales from the Hills,* the hills being the Himalayas. (It was a great success which found an even wider audience when the tales were published individually in the 'Indian Railway' magazine series.) The book's dedication was a diplomatic coup of the first order: 'To the wittiest woman in India.' How many ladies, we may wonder, recognized themselves from this enigmatic description?[27] A number of the themes which were to fascinate Kipling throughout his career appeared in these stories for the first time: flirtation, marital and extra-marital love, hoaxes and revenge, the comic and the supernatural. Few of what Miss J.M.S. Tompkins described as 'barefaced sallies of immature genius', approached the standard he was to attain later, but they were followed in quick succession by other stories, other collections that are outside the scope of this book.

Kipling used what little spare time he could snatch to soak up the atmosphere of the different worlds he inhabited, civil, military and indigenous. As befitted his years, he was impatient of authority and hypocrisy, scoffing, for example, at the Viceroy's staff for being, 'rigidly temperate, Solemn and Serious, prudish and passionless'.[28]

A significant influence on the young writer was Mrs Edmonia ('Ted') Hill, a bright American woman seven years his senior who became his confidante and muse. He composed this witty dedication to her,

---

27 A possible candidate is Isabella, wife to Major General Greaves, on whom the character, Mrs Hauksbee is said to have been based.

28 *Further Information.*

Between the Gum Pot and the Shears,
The weapons of my grimy trade,
In divers moods and various years
These forty foolish yarns were made.

...

Would they were worthier. That's too late -
Cracked pictures stand no further stippling -
Forgive the faults -
    March: 88
To
    Mrs Hill, from Rudyard Kipling.

'The noise which men call fame'

In 1889 the now increasingly successful young author resolved to leave India and make his name in England. (There is talk of a libel action which might have hastened matters.) Armed with six months pay in lieu of notice and money raised by selling some of his publishing rights, Kipling briefly bade farewell to his parents before sailing away, never to live in the Raj again. But the memories did not disappear. Later, in the voice of a time expired soldier sailing home to England, he remembered:

The things that was which I 'ave seen,
In barrick, camp, an' action too,
I tells them over by myself,
An' sometimes wonders if they're true;
For they was odd—most awful odd—
 But all the same now they are o'er,
There must be 'eaps o' plenty such,
An' if I wait I'll see some more.[29]

During a long, lazy voyage 'home', which took in the Far East, America and Canada, Kipling finally landed in Liverpool in October 1889. A train ride away was London, where he established himself in modest rooms in Villiers Street, just off the Strand. It was, he wrote, an

---

29 *'For to Admire'*

area, 'primitive and passionate in its habits and population. My rooms were small, not over-clean or well-kept, but from my desk I could look out of my window through the fanlight of Gatti's Music-Hall entrance, across the street, almost on to its stage.' It embodied, he claimed, 'basic and basaltic truths' about human nature. When the newly created London County Council toyed with the idea of censoring popular entertainment Kipling poured scorn on the proposal.[30] 'What the people of London require[d], he wrote, was 'a poet of the music halls', and he was not above bidding for the title himself. A phrase from one of his songs even went into the language:

> You may make a mistake when you're mashing a tart,
> But you'll learn to be wise when you're older,
> And don't try for things that are out of your reach,
> And that's what the girl told the Soldier, Soldier, Soldier.
> That's what the girl told the Soldier.

At the age of 24 Kipling was a cartoonist's dream with his bushy eyebrows, blue eyes, spectacles and bristling moustache. Up to then, he had not received much critical attention, but all this changed with republication of his short stories the following year. Their novel subject matter and vivid new style caused a considerable stir, contrasting, as they did, with the school of Oscar Wilde and *The Yellow Book*. As a boy, Kipling had admired the 'art for art's sake' philosophy; as a young man who had mixed with members of the Indian civil service and the army, he was repelled by the 'long haired things/in velvet collar rolls/Who talk about the Aims of Art/And "theories" and "goals/And moo and coo with womenfolk/About their blessed souls.'[31] The feeling was mutual; the aesthetes could not comprehend someone like Kipling who was as familiar with the language of the rude soldiery and the working classes as they were alien to them.

Kipling now found himself in the admiring company of such literary giants as Thomas Hardy, Walter Besant, Rider Haggard and Edmund Gosse.

---

30 *Laudatores Actoris Empti.* ?1890.

31 *In Partibus.* (In the land of the unbelievers).

But his friendships extended well beyond the literati. As a keen angler he 'picked up with the shore-end of a select fishing-club, which met in a tobacconist's back-parlour. They were', he wrote, 'mostly small tradesmen, keen on roach, dace and such, but they too had that gift, as I expect their forebears had in Addison's time.'

Not all his new acquaintances were as agreeable. In ways we can only guess at he seems to have fallen into the company of a gang of Left Wingers who,

> '... derided my poor little Gods of the East, and asserted that the British in India spent violent lives 'oppressing' the Native. (This in a land where white girls of sixteen, at twelve or fourteen pounds per annum, hauled thirty and forty pounds weight of bath-water at a time up four flights of stairs!)'

However, it was England itself that was the greatest disappointment. Despite being lionised by the literary establishment Kipling declared himself 'sick of London town/From Shepherds Bush to Bow'.[32] In September 1890 he experienced some sort of breakdown. 'My head has given out and I am forbidden work,' he wrote, '... This is the third time this has happened.' Such troubles fell away when he was introduced to a talented young American literary agent by the name of Wolcott Balestier. A close, even intense, friendship developed between the two men which some have construed - without any evidence whatever - as of a homosexual nature. Such was their friendship that they agreed to cooperate in writing an adventure novel which, when published, was entitled, *The Naulahka. A story of West and East.* (*Naulahka* was an Indian word for 900,000 rupees, in this context a necklace.)

Up to this point, Kipling had had a busy, if not fraught, emotional life. While still in India he had become engaged to more than one young woman. Caroline Taylor (Mrs Hill's sister) was but the latest and she broke it off within months. Fate stepped in the following year when Kipling, now recovering

---

32 *In Partibus.* The poet's reaction against his native country was so severe that Edmund Gosse asked whether there was not in him something of Pagett MP turned inside out. (See the poem of that title below.)

from one of his 'breakdowns', chanced upon his old love, Flo Garrard walking on the Thames embankment. The attraction was rekindled immediately. Now training as a painter, Flo had a relationship with a female fellow student, but continued to see Kipling. The romance was broken off in Paris, possibly for reasons connected with Flo's sexual orientation. (She lives on in elements of the character of Maisie in Kipling's novel, *The Light that Failed.*) It was not long after this that someone else came into his life.

Wolcott Balestier had a sister, Caroline, or 'Carrie', a plain, dark haired teenager with whom Kipling seems to have entered some sort of relationship. It was not one that Kipling's parents approved of. ('A good man spoiled', muttered his father.) It was not an untroubled affair. In August 1891, on medical advice, and possibly because of his confused emotional entanglements, Kipling left England on a tour of the white Dominions. On the way home, while visiting his parents in India, he received a cable from a desperate Carrie which read, 'WOLCOTT DEAD STOP COME BACK TO ME STOP': her brother had died suddenly from typhoid fever while on a business trip to Germany. Kipling's response was a ticket to London and a proposal of marriage.[33] A week later, in what seemed to many to be undue haste, the couple were married by special licence at the fashionable church of All Souls, Langham Place. The novelist Henry James gave the bride away, but the congregation was sparse, the short ceremony taking place in the 'thick of an influenza epidemic, when the undertakers had run out of black horses, and the dead had to be content with brown ones.'[34]

It is said that on his deathbed Wolcott had commended his sister to Kipling's care, but could it have been a coincidence that the two were wed not long after Kipling's final split with Flo Garrard? Is an echo of this to be found in a poem that he was to write decades later?

> Once in life I watched a Star;
> But I whistled, "Let her go!
> There are others, fairer far,

---

33 The proposal may have merely confirmed an earlier, less formal arrangement.
34 *Something of Myself.*

Which my favouring skies shall show."
Here I lied, and herein I
Stood to pay the penalty.[35]

After a honeymoon in Canada the newly married couple started out on a world tour, but it had to be abandoned when the New Oriental Banking Corporation collapsed, taking all Kipling's savings with it. Carrie's family offered them refuge in a simple cottage on the Balestier family estate in Vermont. Here, on a snowy December day in 1892, Carrie gave birth to their first child, Josephine. In the same year Kipling's second collection of verse was published. Entitled *Barrack-Room Ballads and Other Verses*, it was a thumping success, with its sympathetic but un-idealistic portrayal of the British soldier in India. Sir Arthur Quiller Couch, the poet and much respected editor of *The Oxford Book of English Verse*, described the book as containing verse 'for which "splendid" is the only term – so radiantly it glitters with incrustations of barbaric words.'[36] The poet and critic, Lionel Johnson was equally laudatory:

> 'All Mr Kipling's undiverted and undiluted strength has gone into these vivid ballads; phrase follows phrase, instinct with life, quivering and vibrating with the writer's intensity. No superfluity, no misplaced condescension to sentiment, no disguising of things ludicrous or ugly or unpleasant.'[37]

The Kiplings were happy in Vermont and after their second daughter, Elsie was born in 1896 they decided to settle there and bought land outside the town of Brattleboro from Carrie's younger brother, Beatty. Using him as the foreman of works, they built a shingle-style Queen Anne house to Kipling's design, which they named 'Naulakha' after the novel.[38] Rudyard was delighted with the outdoor life, but proud Carrie, whose role in the family the poet recognized by naming her The Committee of Ways and

---

35 *The Penalty*, 1932.

36 *English Illustrated Magazine*, X, No. 120 (Sep. 1893).

37 *The Academy*. May, 1892.

38 Spelled differently from the title of the novel at a time when Indian names had no fixed spellings.

Means, decided that her increasingly successful husband should live in some style, with a carriage and liveried groom; it did little to commend them to their rural neighbours.

But the idyll was not to last; a frontier dispute between Britain and Venezuela gave rise to anti-British sentiment in America. Kipling, who was beginning to have second thoughts about that country, resolved to return to England. Before he could do so, however, an event occurred that was to make their continued stay impossible. Beatty, now the caretaker of 'Naulakha', was a heavy drinker and a spendthrift with 'a tongue like a skinning knife'. He had somehow formed the impression that he had been slandered by Kipling. Meeting his brother-in-law on a country road, he threatened to 'blow out your God-damned brains' if he did not retract his 'Goddam lies'. Kipling had Beatty arrested, but quickly realized his blunder; going to law to settle a personal dispute was utterly inconsistent with the code upon which the future author of 'If-' had based his life.[39] The ensuing trial turned into a farce, with sentiment strongly favouring the local man. Kipling could not bear the embarrassment and fled with his family to England.

They settled first, at Carrie's suggestion, in a rented house in Torquay, but soon came to realize that they liked neither the house nor the area and moved to Rottingdean, where the Burne-Jones's had a holiday home. Another successful collection of verse, *The Seven Seas* now came out. It marked a turning point artistically; while about a third of the poems in the collection dealt with familiar themes, such as India and the British soldier, the rest were concerned with the sea and travel. Not long after, the now vastly successful poet was invited to join the Athenaeum, well below the normal age. (A 'clubby' man, he was also a member of the Carlton, the Savile and the Beefsteak.)

The Kiplings' only son, John was born in 1897. It was also the year of Queen Victoria's Diamond Jubilee, and Kipling crowned the occasion

---

39 When in the short story, *His Private Honour* a young officer struck a private soldier by the name of Ortheris the latter disdained to exercise his right to have his attacker cashiered. 'My rights!', he replied, "'Strewth A'mighty I'm a man."'

with one of his finest poems, the hymn, *Recessional* (not included). It was at about this time that he wrote the following piece of doggerel,

> He's the man who wrote the Jungle Books – likewise The Seven Seas
> He's the man who wrote the private soldier's life –
> He's the man who gets the credit ... but he owns on bended knees,
> He isn't any good without his wife.[40]

In 1898 Kipling took Carrie and the children to South Africa on holiday. It was to be the first of many such visits. As he wrote, 'the children throve, and the colour, light, and half-oriental manners of the land bound chains round our hearts for years to come.' There, Rudyard met and was deeply impressed by Cecil Rhodes, the former prime minister of the Cape Colony. Rhodes' ambition - to see the empire stretch from Cairo to the Cape - struck a chord with the writer, who had been a supporter of the Jameson raid on the Transvaal. (In 1895 a small force of armed police under Dr Leander Starr Jameson had invaded the Boer territory of the Transvaal. It was a failure that ended in imprisonment.) Kipling's Stoic poem, *If-* (not included) was inspired by Jameson.

The following year the family sailed for New York to allow Carrie to see her mother. It was a rough crossing during which both she and Josephine caught colds. Kipling went down with a severe bout of pneumonia in the course of which he was plagued by vivid fantasies.[41] Carrie recovered, only to witness the death of her beloved daughter from pneumonia. She withheld the news from her husband until he regained his health, but the loss hit both of them grievously. For years afterwards, Kipling 'saw' Josephine around their house and garden, an experience which he was to sublimate into the beautiful short story, *They*, and a poignant poem entitled *Merrow Down* (not included), named after a village in Surrey that the family once frequented. Trix was to describe to his surviving daughter,

---

40 *He's the Man who Wrote the Jungle Books.* c. 1896.
41 They are described at length in Kipling's own words in an Appendix to Birkenhead's *Life of Kipling*.

Elsie, how 'after his almost fatal illness & Josephine's death – he was a sadder and harder man.'[42]

Kipling's health continued to trouble him and he was advised to spend his winters abroad. He returned to South Africa, where he took up residence in a house called 'The Woolsack' built for artists like himself by Rhodes, who lived nearby. It was there in a beautiful setting under Table Mountain that he completed his last and finest novel, *Kim*. Set in India against the struggle for regional dominance between Britain and Russia, the story begins at the site of his father's old museum in Lahore, where a young street urchin of mixed blood by the name of Kim is adopted as a disciple by a Tibetan Lama. Their adventures together along India's Grand Trunk Road form the centrepiece to one of the world's great picaresque novels. It was in Pinney's words, 'effectively his farewell to India'.

Relations between the British and the Boer settlers in South Africa had led to hostilities in the early 1880s. They broke out afresh nearly two decades later. Considering that the British army considerably out-numbered an enemy consisting of a civilian militia backed by farmers, its performance in the field was disappointing.[43] Kipling volunteered as a correspondent for a British army newspaper called the *Friend*, briefly coming under fire at the 'Battle' of Kari Siding. And he was outstandingly successful in raising funds to provide comforts for the troops by sales of his poem, *The Absent-minded Beggar* (not included). The British won in the end, but at the cost of a disgraceful death rate caused, in Kipling's view, by 'our own utter carelessness, officialdom and ignorance'.[44] He urged the nation: 'Let us admit it fairly, as a business people should,/We have had no end of a lesson: it will do us no end of good.'[45]

---

42 Ricketts.

43 The Boers had better rifles, better artillery and better tactics (guerrilla warfare). The British responded with a scorched earth policy and concentration camps in which some 30,000 men, women and children died. It was a disaster which Kipling seems to have discounted. ('South Africa' in Something of Myself.)

44 *Something of Myself.*

45 *The Lesson.* (not included).

Sussex by the sea

Back in England, the public came in coach-loads to stare at the great man's home at Rottingdean. It was all too much for someone who valued his privacy, and Kipling started to look elsewhere. In 1902, after some searching, he found and bought a property which was entirely to his liking. It was a Jacobean ironmaster's house called 'Bateman's, just outside the village of Burwash in Sussex. 'Behold us,' he wrote, 'lawful owners of a grey stone, lichened house - A.D.1634 over the door - beamed, panelled, with old oak staircase and all untouched and unfaked.'[46] Three years later he bought an adjacent farm and mill, increasing his acreage to 300. At the age of 32 Kipling was at last settled in the place he was to make his home for the rest of his life.

And he had the means to explore his new kingdom. His first car was an American Locomobile steam car which he described to a friend as 'a holy terror'. Its idiosyncrasies soon led to its being ditched in favour of a Lanchester petrol car, in which Kipling and a succession of chauffeurs roamed the ancient lanes of Sussex and beyond. On one occasion motoring through Northumberland his vehicle suffered a blown tyre, attracting a large crowd. He memorialised the occasion in a pretty piece of verse which began:

> The mind of man it warpeth
> Ay greatly does it warp
> To watch the men of Morpeth
> The godless loons of Morpeth
> Stand round and stare and yawp ... [47]

Kipling was a contented man. England, which not long before he had derided as 'a stuffy little place, mentally, morally and physically', now seemed to him, 'the most wonderful foreign land I have ever been in'. As he wrote in *Sir Richard's Song* (not included):

---

46 Letter to Charles Eliot Norton. Not everyone shared his enthusiasm for this dark and low ceilinged house which lacked a bathroom, running water and electricity.

47 *The Mind of Man it Warpeth.* 1908.

Howso great man's strength be reckoned,
There are two things he cannot flee;
Love is the first and Death is the second ...
And Love in England hath taken me.

And of all England it was Sussex that he loved most, declaring,
I'm just in love with all these three,
The Weald, and the Marsh and the Down Countree,
Nor I don't know which I love the most,
The Weald or the Marsh or the white Chalk coast.[48]

His love of England and its empire was not exclusive. For a time he had admired America and the Americans, but it was an admiration that came and went. His love of France, however, had begun in 1878 when his father had taken him to the Paris Exhibition, where he was in charge of the Indian exhibits. In later years Rudyard took most of his family holidays in that country and addressed two poems of grandiloquent praise to it.[49] His daughter, Elsie told how, while staying at the Hotel Meurice in Paris, the leader of the orchestra asked if there was any piece he would like played. Without hesitation he asked for 'Sambre et Meuse', the stirring march of the French army.

In 1903 a new collection of poems appeared entitled, *The Five Nations*. As well as continuing the military theme, it looked to England as the heart of empire. England and its history were also the subjects of a fine collection of stories and poems entitled *Puck of Pook's Hill* (named after a hill near Bateman's), and, four years later, of a companion volume, *Rewards and Fairies*. Both were in the peculiarly English tradition of work ostensibly written for children but which appeal equally to the adult reader. And they had an unexpected effect. It is not too much to say that, throughout one, possibly two, world wars Kipling's love of England was to inspire its youth to extraordinary efforts without which it, and thus the cause of western civilization, might not have prevailed.

---

48 *A Three part Song.*
49 *'France'* and *'Song of Seventy Horses'.*

Such was the poet's fame that in 1907 his tour of Canada assumed an almost pro-consular character, but by then the forty year old poet had become increasingly out of tune with his times. He had been disillusioned with the Boer settlement and opposed the movement toward Home Rule in Ireland. He had no time for reformist policies, like those of the Liberal government, the moral lapses of which he attacked in his bitter poem, *Gehazi*. Socialist values were even less acceptable. (See *The City of Brass,* not included).

Such concerns fell away however, in 1914 when war with Germany broke out. Kipling toured the country urging young men to join the colours, reinforcing the message with his poem, *For all we have and are*, which ended with the words, 'What stands if Freedom fall?/Who dies if England live?' He also acted as a correspondent for the *Daily Telegraph* in France.

One of those who answered the call was his own eighteen year old son, John who had been educated at Wellington, a school with strong military connections. He was naturally downcast at being rejected by the army on account of bad eyesight and contemplated joining as a ranker. This was too much for his father, who sought the help of his friend, Field Marshal Lord Roberts to secure for his son a temporary commission in the Irish Guards. (There is no truth in the suggestion that Rudyard sent his son unwillingly to war.) Within a few weeks of being posted to France, John's battalion took part in one of those futile offensives designed to create 'the breakthrough' in an essentially static conflict. Like all the others, the assault failed and 8,000 men died in the attempt. Originally posted as 'missing, believed wounded', it soon became clear that John was in fact one of the 385 officers who had perished in the battle of Loos. On hearing the news from his friend, the politician, Andrew Bonar Law, Kipling is said to have uttered a 'curse like the cry of a dying man'. The loss was all the greater since the young man's body was never found in his parents' lifetime.

When the war reached its inconclusive end it gave little comfort to Kipling. As one of the many fathers who had lost a son in the conflict he found some purpose in agreeing to serve as honorary literary adviser to the Imperial (later Commonwealth) War Graves Commission. He threw himself into the task, scrupulously ensuring that Britain's colonial troops should be buried according to their religion. It was he who suggested the words 'Their name liveth for evermore'[50] for the lists of the dead on village memorials, and 'A Soldier of the Great War Known unto God' for the graves of the unidentified. The words, 'The glorious dead' engraved on the cenotaph in Whitehall were his too. His work for the Commission brought the poet into closer contact with King George V, whom he already knew. As a further means of controlling his grief he accepted an invitation to prepare a history of the Irish Guards in the Great War. When it was finished he wrote, 'Never was I so thankful to put a thing behind me'. The task had taxed him severely, but perhaps that was what he was seeking?

The declining years

Britain emerged from the Great War enfeebled and impoverished. Kipling's reacted with a collection of poems entitled *The Years Between*. Its dedication, entitled *The Seven Watchmen*, summed up his belief in trusting to one's own judgement, rather than the dictates of 'authority':

> Seven Watchmen sitting in a tower,
> Watching what had come upon mankind,
> Showed the Man the Glory and the Power,
> And bade him shape the Kingdom to his mind,
> 'All things on Earth your will shall win you.'
> ('Twas so their counsel ran)
> 'But the Kingdom—the Kingdom is within you,'
> Said the Man's own mind to the man.
> For time, and some time -
> As it was in the bitter years before,
> So it shall be in the over-sweetened hour -
> That a man's mind is wont to tell him more
> Than Seven Watchmen sitting in a tower.[51]

---

50 Ecclesiastes, 44: 14.

51 'For a man's soul is sometime wont to bring him tidings; more than seven watchmen that sit on high on a watchtower.' Ecclesiasticus 37, 14.

As with so many men, Kipling's outlook in later life tended toward the reactionary and intolerant, even to the extent of neglecting long lasting friendships. But, then, he had more to bear than most. As well as the loss of a son and a daughter, he had to bear the distress caused by the inter-mittent mental problems of his sister, Trix. On top of this he suffered from abdominal pain, depression and the sleeplessness that so often goes with it. Characteristically, he kept all of this hidden from the world, but hints of his anguish can be detected in some of his most powerful poems of this period, such as *Rahere,* the *Hymn to Physical Pain* and the *Hymn of Breaking Strain.* At the same time his prose became darker and more cryptic, sometimes to the point of obscurity.

For many years Kipling had enjoyed a world-wide reputation. No such consolation was available to his wife who, as well as acting her husband's business manager and housekeeper, had the burden of being gatekeeper to one of the world's most sought-after literary figures. Whatever people thought of her - her only, modest, biography is entitled *The Hated Wife*[52] - Carrie loved her husband and cared for him devotedly to the end, despite crippling rheumatism, diabetes and depression. And of course the loss of their children affected her at least as much as him.

It is a common-place that England slept throughout the inter-war years until 'a quarrel in a far-away country between people of whom we know nothing' unleashed horrors of unimaginable magnitude for the second time in a gen-eration. Kipling was one of the first to sense and warn against the menace.[53] He had used the Asian good luck symbol of the swastika to adorn his books, but when it was adopted as the national flag of Nazi Germany he immedi-ately had it removed, on the ground that it was 'defiled beyond redemption'.[54]

The doctors had never been able to explain Kipling's painful abdominal problem. When in 1921 it was thought to be caused by a disease of the teeth he had them all removed, but to no effect. The symptoms were final-ly diagnosed as those of a duodenal ulcer, but only after the condition was

---

52 By Adam Nicolson.
53 See *The Storm Cone* and *The Bonfires, below.*
54 Letters to friends, 1935.

too advanced to operate on. The ulcer perforated while he and his wife were staying in Brown's hotel, where they had spent their honeymoon night, and he was admitted to the Middlesex Hospital for an emergency operation. It failed, and Kipling died at the age of seventy. Two days later King George V followed him to the grave. 'The King has gone', a newspaper headline proclaimed, 'and taken his trumpeter with him.'[55]

Kipling's ashes are buried in Poets' Corner, Westminster Abbey immediately adjacent to the graves of Hardy and Dickens. Carrie survived her husband by three years and on her death left Bateman's to the National Trust.

---

55 Gilmour.

KIPLING'S REPUTATION

'For my own part I worshipped Kipling at thirteen, loathed him at seventeen, enjoyed him at twenty, despised him at twenty-five and now again rather admire him.'

George Orwell, 1936[56]

'During five literary generations every enlightened person has despised him, and at the end of that time nine-tenths of those enlightened persons are forgotten and Kipling is in some sense still there.'

George Orwell, 1942.[57]

It has been said that Kipling's reputation rose like a rocket and fell like its stick. This was caused in part by fashion. As he wrote,

> Conventions of another age
> Fill us with boredom or with rage
> And that is just how later ages
> Will look upon our dainty pages.[58]

But changes in fashion alone could not account for a fall as dramatic as Kipling's. At one point he had been lauded as the new Dickens; at

---

56 *New English Weekly.* 1936.
57 *Horizon.* 1942
58 'Translation' of Horace, Book IV, 8.

another he was scorned as someone completely out of tune with the times. The odd thing is that, even when he was spurned by the critics, the public never deserted him. As that great stylist, P. G. Woodhouse wrote:

> 'It's odd, this hostility to Kipling. How the intelligentsia do seem to loathe the poor blighter, and how we of the *canaille* revel in his stuff.'[59]

In 1995, to the horror of *The Guardian* newspaper, his poem, *If-* was voted, 'The Nation's Favourite Poem'.[60] But that didn't stop the criticism, some of it of a deeply unpleasant nature.

And it all began so well.

In 1890 a Times leader had compared Kipling with Maupassant.[61] When he arrived in New York nine years later William Dean Howells, 'the dean of American letters', described him as 'the greatest poet in the English speaking world today.' Upon the death of his daughter, Josephine a few months later he received a letter of condolence from the German Kaiser. Kipling's attitude to the Boer war changed all that. As his biographer, Harry Ricketts put it, 'By so earnestly and ostentatiously aligning himself with the British cause in the war – and the set of attitudes that went with it – he had become a sitting target and a figure of fun.'[62] An American journalist asserted that, 'No swifter fall from favor [sic] has been known in literature'.[63] A modest, retiring man, he saw no reason to change his ways, and it was not in his character to defend himself.

---

59 Letter 27 August 1946 published in *Performing Flea*. 1953. For all his success as a humourist, Woodhouse was a literary stylist of the first water.

60 Radio 4 poll.

61 25 March 1890.

62 Edmund Wilson put 'the eclipse' of Kipling's reputation a little later, to 'about 1910'

63 Charles E. Russell. *The Literary Digest*, August 10, 1901.

When the Great War began in 1914 Kipling threw himself once again into the patriotic cause, but as the casualties mounted and the breakthrough which the Allies were striving for failed to materialise public disillusion set in; a disillusion that only deepened after the armistice, when Britain came to count the cost in treasure and in blood.

The post-war years saw a speeding up in the replacement of Victorian values by socialism on the one hand and capitalism on the other; and the masculine ideals of duty and service were pushed aside by suffragism and feminism. Literary styles underwent changes no less radical; nineteenth century romanticism and Georgian poetry were overtaken by Modernism, with its notoriously 'difficult' exponents like T.S. Eliot, Wallace Stevens and Ezra Pound. When Thomas Hardy died in 1928, six of the most celebrated authors of the day helped bear his coffin. Eight years later there was not one professional poet among Kipling's otherwise distinguished pall bearers.

Patriotism made a reappearance with the outbreak of the Second World War, but when it ended Britain found itself further enfeebled, both economically and politically, and its subject peoples could not wait to throw off their yoke. India was 'granted' independence in 1947 and South Africa shrugged off British rule in 1961. Even Canada, Kipling's 'Lady of the Snows', 'patriated' itself from the mother country. The colonies followed hard on the heels of the Dominions, and the empire was effectively done for. As time went by Kipling's fellow countrymen were aware of him only as a children's author, and that by reason of the screen more than the page.[64]

Meanwhile the critics had been lining up against Kipling. In 1941 the distinguished American writer and critic, Edmund Wilson though expressing admiration for the early stories, deplored Kipling's failure to 'mature' into a modern Balzac.[65] (Like other critics before and since, Wilson was criticizing Kipling for not being someone else.) But Kipling was not without powerful admirers, some of them quite unexpected.

---

64 Kipling's stories have been portrayed in such films as *Gunga Din* and *Sergeants Three* (1939), *'The Jungle Books'* (1942 and 1967) and *'The Man Who Would be King'* (1975).

65 The Kipling Nobody Read. *Atlantic Monthly*, 1941.

As early as 1919 the great American[66] essayist, critic and poet, T.S. Eliot had shrugged aside the 'conversational intelligentsia' and acknowledged Kipling as 'a laureate without laurels'.[67] He followed this up in 1941 with a perceptive anthology of Kipling's verse.[68] The most influential part of the book, however was an essay which asserted that, 'no writer has ever cared for the craft of words more than Kipling'. Such praise from so distinguished a Modernist caused a considerable stir in literary circles.

The banner of reappraisal was picked up by the ever perceptive Miss Tompkins in her 1959 analysis of the later stories, and in 1963 by Prof. Rutherford in a collection of critical essays based on his 'conviction that in recent decades Kipling has been too readily, too easily dismissed - that even though adverse judgments must be passed on aspects of his work, his is a more interesting and complex case than has generally been allowed.' It is a reappraisal that is still going on, not only in England, but throughout the world.

Kipling is not widely read in today's India, but he is not without his admirers. The Bengali/English writer, Nirad C. Chaudhuri, for example, described *Kim* as 'the finest novel in the English language with an Indian theme, but also one of the greatest of English novels in spite of the theme.'[69] The Burmese independence hero, Aung San Suu Kyi has written of her admiration for the novel, even naming her second son after its eponymous hero. And the Man Booker prize winner, Suzanna Arundhati Roy once told an inquirer, 'I am an immense fan of Kipling - I could recite him before I could read. I don't necessarily agree with his stated views on India, but I think he was a great writer.'

The praise has not been confined to India. Mark Twain said of his books that they 'never grow pale to me; they keep their colour; they are always

---

66   Eliot became a naturalized Briton in 1927.
67   *Kipling Redivivus*. Review of *The Years Between* in *The Athenaeum*, May, 1919.
68   *A Choice of Kipling's Verse*.
69   T. J. Binyon, *Times Literary Supplement*.

fresh.'[70] Henry James, though quite prepared to criticize his friend, once described him as 'the most complete man of genius (as distinct from fine intelligence) that I have ever known.'[71] James Joyce asserted that, 'the three writers of the nineteenth century who had the greatest natural talents were D'Annunzio, Kipling and Tolstoy.' Ernest Hemingway confessed to a lifelong admiration for Kipling. And the poet, Maya Angelou told how, as a teenage mother in San Francisco, she had been strengthened by his poem, *If-*.

The Argentinean writer, Jorge Luis Borges described Kipling as 'One of the greatest writers.' The German Marxist playwright, Bertolt Brecht drew heavily on his writings. The Russian poet Mikhail Dudin reported that Kipling was very widely read and admired by poets of his generation.[72] And the Trinidadian/British writer, V. S. Naipaul wrote, 'It was all there in Kipling... no writer more honest or accurate, no writer more revealing of himself and society.'

The arguments were summed up in this country by Prof Pinney who in a 1996 essay robustly declared Kipling to have passed the three qualities demanded by Tennyson of a great poet, abundance, variety and complete competence.[73]

All of which leads to the question:

Why was Kipling left out in the cold so long ?

Paradoxically, one reason for Kipling going out of fashion was his popular success. Prof. Norman Page put his finger on it when he wrote, 'Such items as "Shillin a day" and "Gunga Din" were favourite recitation pieces

70 *Hello Goodbye Hello: A Circle of 101 Remarkable Meetings,* Craig Brown.

71 Letter to William James, 6 February 1892.

72 Katherine Hodgson. *The Poetry of Rudyard Kipling in Soviet Russia.*

73 *In Praise of Kipling.* College of Liberal Arts, Harry Ransom Humanities Research Center, University of Texas at Austin (1996).

for so long that it is easy to suppose that they were no more than colourful and vigorous, if somewhat crude and brash light verse, and that they owed their huge popularity to a combination of exotic subject matter, catchy rhythms and comic Cockney dialect.'[74] As Pinney wrote, Kipling was so quotable that he dwindled into cliché.[75]

But familiarity can do no more than push a poet or a style of poetry into obscurity: this was not the case with Kipling. He was not merely ignored, but made the object of scorn and derision. He has at different times been described as an elitist, a chauvinist, a militarist and a paternalist. Even the normally level headed George Orwell once condemned him as 'morally insensitive and aesthetically disgusting'.[76] It's fairly strong stuff and the reason for it seems to be that Kipling offended two powerful streams of thought, the political and the aesthetic. The first condemned him for his political incorrectness, the second for following his own innovative path instead of bowing to contemporary literary fashions.

Kipling cherished his privacy and loathed the crowd, an attitude which some saw as elitist and some, anti-democratic. He was, it is true, a life-long Tory, but his political views were never fully thought out and were often inconsistent, resembling a private morality more than a political. As Gilmour wrote, '[He] was a Conservative with a capital C but he was not a Blimpish reactionary. He preferred Tory policies to Liberal ones on questions of empire, defence and taxation, but he was not a squire lamenting the passing of the eighteenth century ...'

He had as little time for political theory as for party politics, turning down the offer of a Parliamentary seat more than once. As the late Philip Mason observed, 'it would be absurd to regard Kipling [or any poet, the present editor would add] as a political philosopher'. His only venture into this territory was in drawing up, along with Julian Ralph, what the pair of them described as the 'British Principles'. It was no more than a statement of centre

---

74 Page, *A Kipling Companion*.
75 Thomas Pinney, 'Kipling, (Joseph) Rudyard (1865–1936)', *Oxford Dictionary of National Biography*, Oxford University Press, 2004; online edn, Jan 2011.
76 Orwell. *Horizon*. February 1942.

right libertarianism.[77] At the heart of it was what lawyers call the rule of law, or in Kipling's wonderful words, 'Ancient Right unnoticed as the breath we draw—/Leave to live by no man's leave, underneath the Law'.[78]

Evelyn Waugh may have had the measure of Kipling's political outlook when he described him as 'a conservative in the sense that he believed civilization to be something laboriously achieved which was only precariously defended. He wanted to see the defences fully manned and he hated the liberals because he thought them gullible and feeble, believing in the easy perfectibility of man and ready to abandon the work of centuries for sentimental qualms.'[79]

To understand Kipling one must remember that he began his working life at the height of empire. He lived at the heart of it, and he believed firmly in the best of it. But he was far from being a jingoist. When in one of the *Stalky & Co* stories[80] a politician, visiting the semi-fictional college, sought to wrap himself metaphorically in the Union flag, the boys' leader condemned him as 'an outrageous stinker, a jelly-bellied flag-flapper.' To Kipling, the empire was the white man's *burden*, a duty to be discharged not a privilege to be enjoyed. '[My] concept of empire', he once wrote, 'was that which I saw around me – men devoted to burdensome tasks under difficult conditions without much assistance or any immediate hope of reward, working for impersonal ends.'[81] His was not an uncritical fealty: whenever his countrymen fell short of the high standards he set for them he used his talents to expose their failures, even when it brought

---

77 The Principles were: '1. The absolute independence of the individual, so long as he does not interfere with his neighbour's rights 2. Prompt and equal justice, before the Lord, to all men 3. A natural and rooted antipathy to anything savouring of military despotism, in any shape or form 4. Absolute religious toleration and freedom of belief for all peoples 5. Prompt and incorruptible justice to all men in every walk of life, and 6. The right of every man to make his home his castle.' (2 and 5 would seem to overlap somewhat.)

78 *'The Old Issue'*, 1899. This couplet is still quoted by jurists on both sides of the Atlantic.

79 *The Essays, Articles and Reviews of Evelyn Waugh*, 22 March 1964.

80 *The Flag of their Country.*

81 Letter to friend. Kipling Papers 25/3.

him only grief.[82] In his deeply moving hymn, *Recessional* Kipling warned the English to reflect upon the transience of empire, to avoid the temptations of power and the boastings of the proud. In *The Islanders* he bitterly condemned the governing class, and in *The Old Guard,* the officer class. They were not poems designed to make friends among the establishment.

Kipling had seen how in South Africa British lack of foresight had led to military disaster and needless death. In the years leading up to the Great War his pleas for preparedness were seen as bellicosity. (Similar slurs were cast against Churchill in 1945.) When Armageddon finally arrived, as Kipling had warned it would, many, like Rupert Brooke, welcomed it with unseemly enthusiasm. Kipling on the other hand evinced only the grim realism of someone who knew what was in store:

> 'Our world has passed away
> In wantonness o'erthrown.
> There is nothing left to-day
> But steel and fire and stone!'[83]

Orwell must be credited for pointing to the difference of style between Tennyson's *The Charge of the Light Brigade:*

> "Forward the Light Brigade!"
> Was there a man dismay'd?
> Not though the soldier knew
> Someone had blunder'd.

and the realism of Kipling's poem, *The 'eathen:*

> An' now the hugly bullets come peckin' through the dust,
> An' no one wants to face 'em, but every beggar must;
> So, like a man in irons, which isn't glad to go,
> They moves 'em off by companies uncommon stiff an' slow.'

---

82   As in his poem, *The Islanders* which condemned the 'the flannelled fools at the wicket' and 'the muddied oafs at the goals' for failing their country.

83   *For all we have and are.*

More serious than the charge of jingoism is the hoary old calumny of racialism that the present editor is embarrassed at having to refute yet again. How could someone be a white racist whose first loves were India and its peoples? In his finest novel the eponymous hero is asked, 'And who are thy people, O Friend of all the World?'

> 'This great and beautiful land,' said Kim, waving his hand round the little clay-walled room where the oil-lamp in its niche burned heavily through the tobacco-smoke.'

The poet, Craig Raine has pointed to the, 'critics [who] have stopped, affronted, at the first stanza [of *The White Man's Burden*]: "Your new-caught, sullen peoples,/Half-devil and half child."[84] Whereas, the last three stanzas make clear that 'the judgment of the colonised on the colonisers will be the judgment of equals, "the judgment of your peers."' Similarly, the reference in *Recessional* to 'lesser breeds without the law' has, in Orwell's words, '[a]lways [been] good for a snigger in pansy-left circles'. In fact it is lifted from Romans, 2.14 which refers to the Gentiles (or non-Jews) as a people 'having not the law', in other words it is a generic term for outsiders, in that context the Germans.

Even sillier is the denigration which has been directed at *The Ballad of East and West*. The first line, 'Oh. East is East and West is West and never the twain shall meet' (a statement of fact about nineteenth century Indian society[85]) must, of course, be balanced by the last, '... there is neither East nor West, Border, nor Breed, nor Birth,/When two strong men stand face to face though they come from the ends of the earth!' The poet's point was that character can overcome even the bonds of convention.

Some have condemned a remark in one of Kipling's letters in which he described his Indian newspaper colleagues as 'touchy as children, obstinate

---

84 Following a war with America the United States of America had effectively annexed the Philippine islands and Kipling was urging them to follow a humanitarian path towards their subject peoples.

85 See Prof. Janusz Buda's *The Ballad of East and West*. Otsuma Women's University Faculty of Literature Annual Report, Vol. XVIII.

as men.' He was prone to make similar criticisms of Americans; an error, maybe, but hardly a sign of racism. In any event the rest of the letter tends to be ignored:

> 'the proper way to handle 'em is not by looking on 'em 'as excitable masses of barbarism' (I speak for the Punjab only) or the 'down trodden millions of Ind groaning under the heel of an alien and unsympathetic despotism', but as men with a language of their own which it is your business to understand; and proverbs which it is your business to quote (this is a land of proverbs) and bywords and allusions which it is your business to master; and feelings which it is your business to enter into and sympathize with.' [86]

Even in the 1930s Kipling had very real doubts about the ability of Indians to govern themselves, but he was not afraid of what we now call diversity. In *Something of Myself* he recorded how,

> 'In '85 I was made a Freemason by dispensation (Lodge Hope and Perseverance 782 E.C.), being under age, because the Lodge hoped for a good Secretary... Here I met Muslims, Hindus, Sikhs, members of the Araya and Brahmo Samaj, and a Jewish Tyler, who was a priest and butcher to his little community in the city. So yet another world was opened to me which I needed.'[87]

Criticism has sometimes been misdirected at his poem, *The Stranger*, which begins,

The Stranger within my gate,
He may be true or kind,
But he does not talk my talk -
I cannot feel his mind.
I see the face and the eyes and the mouth,
But not the soul behind.

---

86 Craig Raine. Kipling: Controversial Questions, in *Kipling Journal*, September, 2002.
87 The diverse racial composition alluded to in his poem, *The Mother Lodge* (not included) seems to have been an aspiration rather than reality, but that does not affect the sentiment.

It should be obvious that these words were not intended to represent the author's view, but were the poet's attempt to put himself in another man's sandals: the poem is a clear condemnation of moral blindness. Anyone doubting this need only compare it with another of his pieces, *Hadramauti*, which seeks to portray a 'pagan's' view. It begins,

> Who knows the heart of the Christian? How does he reason?
> What are his measures and balances? Which is his season
> For laughter, forbearance or bloodshed, and what devils move him
> When he arises to smite us? *I* do not love him.

Does this mean that Kipling was anti-Western?

Kipling was certainly *sans pareil*, but he was not *sans reproche*. Sometimes a spirit of vengefulness could descend upon him when contemplating those he scorned, like the German Kaiser whom he saw as responsible for the brutalities of the Great War.[88] The spirit manifested itself in a few bitter stories and poems, sometimes disguised under the cloak of humour.

It would be good to be able to say that Kipling did not share the low level anti-Semitism that was widespread in Britain right up until the end of the Second World War; but he did, elliptically in his writings and, more overtly, in his private communications. But this should be recognized for what it was, a failure to reject the assumptions of his class and time. On the other hand, as Angus Wilson pointed out, 'again and again in his work [he] expresses his respect for the Jewish contribution to Western civilization.'

These blemishes in Kipling's character cannot be defended, but they must be weighed against his merits, including his portrayal of the ethical dilemmas, inconsistencies and ambiguities which beset us all. (See for example, his wonderful poem, *Mary Pity Women*.) Equally important is his concern for the oppressed, whether the 'weaker sex' (*'For the Women'*), prisoners (*'The Captive'*, *'The Song of the Galley Slaves'*), oppressed minorities (*'A Pict Song'*), exiles (*'The Broken Men'*), the

---

88 The jury is still out on the Kaiser's role in the war.

undervalued (*'Chant-Pagan'*), or misfits of any stripe (*'Gentlemen-Rankers'*). When officialdom averted its eyes from the poor and hungry peasantry of India he berated them in an angrily mocking poem which gave great offence to those at whom it was directed.[89] As Craig Raine wrote, 'the discovery for literature of the underdog is a bent which determined the arc of Kipling's career'.[90]

Before Kipling, no one had written so extensively or so sympathetically of 'the mere uncounted folk [of England]/Of whose life and death is none/Report or lamentation'.[91] In 1965 a contributor to *Marxism Today* affirmed, 'There is no other considerable writer, except Hugh McDiarmid, who has written or attempted to write poetry in working class language; it is a pity that the left-wing poets of the thirties ... made no attempt to study his methods... He had a profound sense of history, and therefore of change and development, but his history was always human, and human of the common people; never of kings and aristocrats.'[92]

Martin Fido offered an ingenious reconciliation of this complex character:

> 'Kipling, as we think of him, was shaped by Anglo-Indian official and military society. And this society was predominantly philistine and provincial: deeply racist, anti-democratic, and politically anti-liberal. Kipling, of course, had developed during his boyhood strong reserves of aestheticism, metropolitanism, humanity, friendliness across class-barriers, and generosity, which prevented these vices from corrupting his art. But he was infected by them, and defended them, for they were attitudes held by a society which he knew to be superciliously undervalued by the centres of artistic power.'[93]

---

89 See *The Masque of Plenty* below.
90 *London Review of Books,* August 1992.
91 See his poem, *The Charm,* below.
92 Jack Dunman. August 1965.
93 Fido, Martin. *Rudyard Kipling.*

But I doubt that this is a full answer. As Prof. Pinney sagely observed, 'The contrast ... in Kipling's life between the stridency of his political views and the wide sympathy of his work shows how little we understand the relations of politics to literature.'[94]

Kipling was a modest man. Though he accepted the Nobel Prize for Literature in 1907, the first Englishman to do so, he rejected his own country's highest honours. He indicated that, if offered, he would not accept the Poet Laureateship (which went to the relative nonentity, Alfred Austen[95]). He is believed to have twice refused a knighthood and thrice declined the coveted Order of Merit.[96] However, the man who was judged to be unqualified for Oxford was pleased to accept a number of honorary doctorates, and in 1922 was elected Lord Rector of Edinburgh University. This post, which involved cultivating the minds of the young, seems to have given him considerable satisfaction.[97]

Kipling's high standing as a novelist and short story writer is now well recognized; it is time to consider the merits of his poetry.

94   Pinney. DNB.

95   Upon Austen's death in 1913 the Laureateship was not offered to Kipling on the ground that he was likely to refuse it again.

96   Kipling gave voice to his lack of interest in such honours in his ballad, *The Last Rhyme of True Thomas*.

97   See *A Rector's Memory* below.

KIPLING THE POET

'The Devil whispered behind the leaves, "It's pretty but is it art?"'

The Conundrum of the Workshop

Kipling was a craftsman like his father, but with words instead of the brush or the chisel. As well as being extraordinarily well-read, he had a remarkably wide vocabulary. 'Who else,' wrote the novelist and poet, George Moore, 'except Whitman, has written the whole language since the Elizabethans?'[98] This is how Kipling described his method of working:

> 'I made my own experiments in the weights, colours, perfumes, and attributes of words in relation to other words, either as read aloud so that they may hold the ear, or, scattered over the page, draw the eye. There is no line of my verse or prose which has not been mouthed till the tongue has made all smooth, and memory, after many recitals, has mechanically skipped the grosser superfluities.'[99]

The result was what Kipling's contemporary, the American critic, Charles Eliot Norton described as the poet's 'frequent perfect mating of word with sentiment, the graphic epithet, the force, freedom, directness, and simplicity of diction, the exquisite movement and flow of rhythm, the felicity of rhyme.'[100] He certainly had a remarkable power to choose the

---

98   Moore. *Avowals.*
99   *Something of Myself.*
100   Norton. *Atlantic Monthly,* 1897.

right word, to turn the right phrase. ('If you can keep your head when all about you', 'the female of the species', 'east is east and west is west', 'the law of the jungle', 'the white man's burden', and so on). Once minted, many of them have lingered in the popular imagination; sometimes, as suggested above, to the detriment of his other work.

But can what he wrote properly be described as poetry? This odd sounding question must be taken seriously because it was posed by none other than T.S. Eliot. In his seminal essay of 1941 Eliot concluded that Kipling, 'does write poetry, but that is not what he is setting out to do.'[101] It was almost as if he was suggesting that the poet somehow achieved poetry *malgré lui*.

It was Kipling himself who started the hare when in *Something of Myself* he insisted on applying the term, 'verse' to all his poetic output. The word has dangerous overtones, hinting, as it does, at a level of skill inferior to 'poetry proper'. In his densely argued essay, Eliot explained that in describing Kipling's output as 'verse' he implied no value judgement. 'I can,' he wrote, 'think of a number of poets who have written great poetry, only of a very few whom I should call great verse writers. And unless I am mistaken, Kipling's position in this class is not only high, but unique.' A compliment, certainly, but it is difficult to agree with the implication that Kipling's 'verse' is necessarily and in some less than fully explained way inferior, for example, to lyric poetry. It would, as Craig Raine observed, be a strange definition of poetry which would exclude Pope and Dryden.

As a young man in India Kipling certainly wrote verse in the sense of metrical lines of no great literary merit; more substantial achievements were to come later. Take for example the seemingly straightforward, *Alnaschar and the Oxen* (1926), which ends,

> There's a valley, under oakwood, where a man may dream his dream,
> In the milky breath of cattle laid at ease,
> Till a moon o'ertops the alders, and her image chills the stream,
> And the river-mist runs silver round their knees!

---

101 *A Choice of Kipling's Verse.*

Now the footpaths fade and vanish; now the ferny clumps deceive;
Now the hedgerow-folk possess their fields anew;
Now the Herd is lost in darkness, and I bless them as I leave,
My Sussex Cattle feeding in the dew!

Kipling had no qualms about using verse for didactic purpose. 'It would not seem', Dobrée wrote of such poems, 'that there is anything like them in the language.' 'Much of what [he] wrote,' he added, 'vexed the world, sometimes by its direct attack on its complacency, but more importantly ... by forcing the individual to face himself, the conditions of living, or the abyss of darkness which he sometimes feels may engulf him.' Didactic verse, it is true, can sometimes lapse into the humdrum or the ponderous, but this was an error that Kipling fell into only rarely. As he himself observed of writers,

'Unless they please they are not heard at all.'[102]

Kipling's mastery of technique permitted him to explore an unusually broad range of poetic form in a way Kingsley Amis described as without parallel in our language. While conceding his weaknesses, Dobrée has described how '[h]e was at home in the heroic couplet, common measure, ballad forms; the iambic or the rollicking anapaest as well as more difficult prosodic units; the octosyllabic or the sixteener, literally 'free' verse, though rhymed; a variation of the *terza rima*, the varied seventeenth century stanza, or something too readily regarded as Swinburnian, though dating from much earlier.' He even wrote a 'Chinese' poem after the style of Arthur Waley.[103] 'There are,' as Kipling himself wrote, 'nine and sixty ways of constructing tribal lays,/And every single one of them is right!'[104]

Kipling's authorised biographer, Charles Carrington explained how, 'When the substance of a poem was forming in [Kipling's] mind he found a tune - not a metre but a tune - and absorbed himself in its rhythm until

---

102 *The Fabulists.*
103 *Arterial.*
104 *In the Neolithic Age.*

the words arranged themselves, whereupon the poem was made.' That was why Kipling turned, more frequently than any other medium, to song and the ballad. Both are easy on the ear and demand no special literary training to enjoy. However, in the hands of a great talent like Kipling's, I suggest, simplicity of form or language does not necessarily imply simplicity of meaning or lack of intensity. 'It is', as Dobrée wrote, 'only the high finish of his art that makes him seem to lack subtlety'.[105] Even his critics have to concede that, whatever verse form Kipling employed, the result usually lingers in the mind.

Marghanita Laski observed that, 'In few writers – only Dickens comes to mind – is the gap between best and worst so wide. It is as if different men were at work; and so in a sense, they were.'[106] Those anxious to discover the poet at his worst must look elsewhere because the poems in this anthology are chosen from among his best - though not all the best are included, both for want of space and for the reasons given in the Preface.

For all his stuffy image Kipling was a great innovator. Since the days of Dickens, the poor spoke seldom on the page and always in perfect English. Kipling's practice of putting regional, or demotic, English into the mouths of private soldiers and working class folk was a great novelty at the time, but it was one that did not always please. Orwell suggested that, 'Very often the result is as embarrassing as the humorous recitation at a church social'. (Or, one might add, some of Shakespeare's comic interludes.) On re-reading the 'Soldiers Three' stories, where three strong dialects collide, the present editor sees some force in his point, but finds no such difficulty with the poems, which still seem to him to be fair representations of the soldier speech he once knew.

Another of his innovations was the use at the head of his stories, of an epigraph, or a poem designed to complement the tale. The epigraphs were often imaginatively successful, but not always. Some were written for the purpose, others were not. Some were very much to the point; the

---

105 Dobrée. *The Lamp and the Lute: Studies in Seven Authors.*
106 Laski. *From Palm to Pine. Rudyard Kipling Abroad and at Home.*

relevance of others can be made out only with difficulty. The enjoyment of most of the epigraphs can be improved by reading the story to which they were attached; the opposite is not always true.

A characteristic of both Kipling's prose and poetry was his love of the English countryside, which in turn informed his love of English history, most notably in the *Puck* stories and their accompanying poems. These have sometimes been criticized for their lack of historical accuracy. It is a fair point: he was not an historian. What he did possess, however, was an affection for the past and a desire to explore how it fashioned his today. For many, such as Marghanita Laski and the present editor, the results have enhanced their appreciation of our island's story. As he once told the Royal Society of Literature, 'Fiction is Truth's elder sister. No one in the world knew what truth was until someone had told a story.'[107] The greatly respected historian, G.M. Trevelyan impliedly supported this view when he wrote, 'As a piece of historical imagination I know nothing in the world better than the third story in *Puck* called *The Joyous Venture* ... I can see no fault in it and many a merit.' Against such praise, the poet may perhaps be pardoned for his occasional infelicities.

In fact, Kipling's history was oftentimes surprisingly accurate, as for example in his metrical summary of clause 29 of the Magna Carta.[108] (Try doing that with any other piece of mediaeval legislation!) He achieved a similar success when he outlined for children the most peculiar character of the first of the Stuart kings in a poem entitled *James I*.[109]

---

107 Speech to the Centenary Banquet of the Royal Society of Literature, 7 July, 1926.

108 'At Runnymede, at Runnymede,/Your rights were won at Runnymede! /No freeman shall be fined or bound,/Or dispossessed of freehold ground,/Except by lawful judgment found/And passed upon him by his peers./Forget not, after all these years,/The Charter signed at Runnymede. (*What say the Reeds at Runnymede?*)

109 'The child of Mary Queen of Scots,/A shifty mother's shiftless son,/Bred up among intrigues and plots,/Learnèd in all things, wise in none./Ungainly, babbling, wasteful, weak,/Shrewd, clever, cowardly, pedantic,/The sight of steel would blanch his cheek./The smell of baccy drive him frantic./He was the

Objection has been made to Kipling's use of archaisms and 'poetic' words, a practice which had begun to disappear at the beginning of the twentieth century. When one of his American correspondents mildly chided him for this he snapped back: '"thro'" and "kist" are POETRY. ... Also t's make past participles snappier at their ends.'[110] The present editor finds no problem with this practice, but, then, he is of an older generation.

Like most artists, Kipling poured his own character and life experiences into his art. But he also used the creatures of his imagination to explore personalities and attitudes utterly alien to his own, often so skillfully that it is impossible to be sure where the art ends and the man begins. Was he the egalitarian of *Jobson's Amen* or the mob hater of *The Coin Speaks,* the misogynist of *The Female of the Species* or the woman defender of *For the Women*? Was he the compassionate reconciliator of *The Burden* or the author of the deeply unpleasant, *A Death Bed.*[111] Or was he merely a poet trying to inhabit the minds of other men? There is no simple answer to these questions. Kipling, who was fascinated by St Paul, once put these words into the mouth of the apostle:

> I am made all things to all men –
> In City or Wilderness
> Praising the crafts they profess
> That some may be drawn to the Lord ...[112]

There are, as Angus Wilson put it, 'great contradictions and evasions here as in all ... he said and did.' And his poetry was the greater for it.

---

author of his line –/He wrote that witches should be burnt;/He wrote that monarchs were divine,/And left a son who – proved they weren't!'

110   Letter to Brander Matthews. 29 November 1921.

111   Not included here. However, the poem appears as one of the half dozen by Kipling that find a place in the latest edition of the *Oxford Book of English Verse*. There's no accounting for taste.

112   *At his execution*. 1932. The first line is taken directly from Corinthians 9.25.

Kipling used his high poetic skills and unequalled command of language to draw attention to the sufferings of the underdog of all colours, classes and genders, to lift the veil on the pity of war and the pain of the soul. In doing so he added to the sum of wisdom, honesty and tolerance in the corpus of English poetry.

THE ANTHOLOGY

The poems in this anthology have been selected in accordance with the principles set out in the Preface.

For the text I have relied on Prof. Pinney's magisterial, Cambridge Edition of the Poems of Rudyard Kipling (2013), *eschewing only the use of block capitals for the titles. Where a date is not associated in that work with the text I have added it at the end in square brackets.*

I have elected to group the poems under themes that interested the author. The Kipling Society lists some 100 of them, which is far too many for this little work, so I have adopted a simplified classification and ask the reader's pardon if my taxonomy does not always please. Within those themes the poems appear in order of publication.

Each poem is prefaced by a few background notes of my own. For a fuller textual analysis, readers are referred to the Kipling Society's New Readers' Guide, available free to all on the internet.

THE THEMES

Men and women
>Vers de société
>Love and marriage

The burden of empire
>Rome
>India
>Work, duty and 'the law'

War and the soldier
>A soldier's life
>Afghanistan
>The pity of war
>Returning from the wars

Healing

Exploration and discovery
>Technology and the sea
>The wide world o'er

England

Storytelling

The greathearted

Faith and the numinous

Magic and mystery

Teacher and prophet

Autobiographical

MEN AND WOMEN

'... the wildest dreams of Kew are the facts of Khatmandhu,
And the crimes of Clapham chaste in Martaban.'
In the Neolithic Age

Even as a young man Kipling possessed the chameleon art of inhabiting the minds of others, whether caught in an idle moment or experiencing the deeper joys and tragedies of life. Many of the poems from his time as a journalist in India were based on real characters, actual events: it did not always win him friends. David Gilmour quotes one lady as saying, 'in Simla the writer was considered a cad, a bounder, and a subversive pamphleteer given to criticise his betters.'

VERS DE SOCIÉTÉ

Despite the fact that they were rejected by T.S. Eliot in his celebrated anthology of Kipling's verse, I begin with three examples of the fluent, witty verse of the poet's early years, because they laid the first bricks of his reputation.

And because they are *fun*.

Philip Mason, who was more familiar than most with the life and manners of the British Raj, described how at the time of Kipling's literary apprenticeship, 'not only did "senior ladies" quarrel over the right to go into dinner first, but men fought for the favours of women who were witty and self-possessed.'

The ball was the principal occasion upon which young women could legitimately encounter, even touch, young men. The narrator in the following poem was based on Kipling's daughter, Alice, whose age she fitted exactly.

My Rival

I go to concert, party, ball—
      What profit is in these?
I sit alone against the wall
      And strive to look at ease.
The incense that is mine by right
      They burn before Her shrine;
And that's because I'm seventeen
      And She is forty-nine.

I cannot check my girlish blush,
      My color comes and goes;
I redden to my finger-tips,
      And sometimes to my nose.
But She is white where white should be,
      And red where red should shine.
The blush that flies at seventeen
      Is fixed at forty-nine.

I wish I had Her constant cheek;
      I wish that I could sing
All sorts of funny little songs,
      Not quite the proper thing.
I'm very *gauche* and very shy,
      Her jokes aren't in my line;
And, worst of all, I'm seventeen
      While She is forty-nine.

The young men come, the young men go
      Each pink and white and neat,
She's older than their mothers, but
      They grovel at Her feet.
They walk beside Her 'rickshaw-wheels -
      None ever walk by mine;
And that's because I'm seventeen
      And She is forty-nine.

She rides with half a dozen men,
      (She calls them "boys" and "mashes")
I trot along the Mall alone;
      My prettiest frocks and sashes
Don't help to fill my programme-card,
      And vainly I repine
From ten to two A.M. Ah me!
      Would I were forty-nine!

She calls me "darling," "pet," and "dear,"
      And "sweet retiring maid."
I'm always at the back, I know, -
      She puts me in the shade.
She introduces me to men, -
      "Cast" lovers, I opine,
For sixty takes to seventeen,
      Nineteen to forty-nine.

But even She must older grow
      And end Her dancing days,
She can't go on forever so
      At concerts, balls and plays.
One ray of priceless hope I see
      Before my footsteps shine;
Just think, that She'll be eighty-one
      When I am forty-nine!
[1885]

The tale of Jack Barrett was, according to Ricketts, 'a thinly disguised version of a topical scandal.' The contemporary reader should be warned that in Kipling's time the word, 'screw' was a slang term for salary.

Quetta is some 800 miles from Simla by road.

The Story of Uriah

'Now there were two men in one city; the one rich and the other poor'.

2 Samuel xii. 1.

Jack Barrett went to Quetta
    Because they told him to.
He left his wife at Simla
    On three-fourths his monthly screw.
Jack Barrett died at Quetta
    Ere the next month's pay he drew.

Jack Barrett went to Quetta.
    He didn't understand
The reason of his transfer
    From the pleasant mountain-land.
The season was September,
    And it killed him out of hand.

Jack Barrett went to Quetta
    And there gave up the ghost,
Attempting two men's duty
    In that very healthy post;
And Mrs. Barrett mourned for him
    Five lively months at most.

Jack Barrett's bones at Quetta
    Enjoy profound repose;
But I shouldn't be astonished
    If *now* his spirit knows

The reason of his transfer
    From the Himalayan snows.

And, when the Last Great Bugle Call
    Adown the Hurnai throbs,
And the last grim joke is entered
    In the big black Book of Jobs.
And Quetta graveyards give again
    Their victims to the air,
I shouldn't like to be the man
    Who sent Jack Barrett there.

[1886]

LOVE AND MARRIAGE

Young men will write embarrassing love poems as surely as the sun rises and sets; which is exactly what Kipling seems to have done endlessly at the age of 17. Many, but not all, were addressed to his childhood love, Flo Garrard. The following extract is characteristic of them, both in its talent and in its ability to embarrass.

Now that I have accomplished a little,
Very little truly, but still a little –
Made, painfully some, joyfully others, bitterly many, -
Made, as a boy makes them, - imperfect meaning to be perfect.
Failures many, but telling of what was intended,
They are yours and yours only –
By the power and the dominance that you have over me,
Yours and yours only.[113]

---

113 *An Ending. 1882*

And this is one of the better poems of this period.

Understanding

One time when ashen clouds received the sun
     And the sea rose beneath us, clamouring
And the wind's wrath, and the day was almost done
     We met upon the levels, and heard sing
A little mother lark - and found her nest
     Among the sodden hedges, while above,
She poured us from the treasury of her breast
     [...]
And for an instant both our hearts were stirred
     To the same music, and our souls were one
And to her lips my own hot lips were set -
     Then close behind us dropped the mother bird,
And either heart drew back to dwell alone -
     And bitterly each soul cried out 'Not Yet'. -

[1882]

The next poem deals, not with love, but with its close relative, passion. It was based on a press report of April 1883 that 'A native woman was found this afternoon, lying with her throat cut, in the compound of the Civil and Military Gazette Office. The police are endeavouring to find some clue to the murder.'

The description of the dead body and its surroundings is so explicit, so colourful that one wonders whether the poet, who was then working at the CMG, might have witnessed the moment when 'Life's last flicker leaves her countenance'.

A Murder in the Compound

At the wall's foot a smear of fly-flecked red -
    Discoloured grass wherefrom the wild bees flee.
Across the pathway to the flower-bed,
    The dark stream struggles forward, lazily,
Blackened by that fierce fervour overhead
She does not heed, to whom the noontide glare
    And the flies' turmoil round her livid lips
Are less account than that green puddle where,
    Just out of reach, the turbid water slips
Between the corn-ridge and the *siris* trees ...
    The crows are gathered now, and peer and glance
Athwart the branches, and no passer sees,
    When Life's last flicker leaves her countenance.
How, merrily, they drop down, one by one,
To that gay-tinted bundle in the sun.

[1883]

Amour de Voyage *dates from the nineteen year old author's voyage to India on board the* Brindisi. *An academic has criticized its 'world-weary cynicism' as 'an unlikely and unattractive posture for a nineteen-year-old to assume', but this is exactly the attitude young men of that age are disposed to adopt – and Kipling does it so deftly.*

Amour de Voyage

And I was a man who could write you rhyme
       (Just so much for you, nothing more),
And you were the woman I loved for a time -
       Loved for a little, and nothing more.
We shall go our ways when the voyage is o'er,
       You with your beauty and I with my rhymes,
With a dim remembrance rising at times
       (Only a memory, nothing more)
Of a lovely face and some worthless rhymes.

Meantime till our comedy reaches its end
       (It's comic ending, and nothing more)
I shall live as your lover who loved as a friend -
       Shall swear true love till life be o'er.
And you, you must make believe and attend,
       As the steamer throbs from shore to shore.

And so, we shall pass the time for a little
       (Pass it in pleasure, and nothing more),
For vows, alas! are sadly brittle,
       And each may forget the oaths that we swore.
And have we not loved for an age, and age?
       And was I not yours from shore to shore?
From landing-stage to landing-stage
       Did I not worship and kneel and adore?
And what is a month in love but an age?
       And who in their senses would wish for more?

[1885]

Blue Roses is a more lyrical and, I believe, more successful reflection upon love (though Marghanita Laski believed it was written 'as a skit'). Like the previous poem, it was addressed to Florence Garrard.

Blue Roses

> Roses red and roses white
> Plucked I for my love's delight.
> She would none of all my posies -
> Bade me gather her blue roses.
>
> Half the world I wandered through,
> Seeking where such flowers grew.
> Half the world unto my quest
> Answered me with laugh and jest.
>
> Home I came at wintertide,
> But my silly love had died,
> Seeking with her latest breath
> Roses from the arms of Death.
>
> It may be beyond the grave
> She shall find what she would have.
> Mine was but an idle quest -
> Roses white and red are best!

[1887]

At some time or another love, for most of us, is ineluctably yoked with grief. Rather poignantly, a copy of the next poem was discovered in the handwriting of Kipling's mother, Alice, dated July, 1910.[114] Her husband died early the following year.

The Widower

For a season there must be pain -
For a little, little space
I shall lose the sight of her face,
Take back the old life again
While She is at rest in her place.

For a season this pain must endure,
For a little, little while
I shall sigh more often than smile
Till Time shall work me a cure,
And the pitiful days beguile.

For that season we must be apart,
For a little length of years,
Till my life's last hour nears,
And, above the beat of my heart,
I hear Her voice in my ears.

[1890]

---

114 Pinney.

Seal Lullaby, *or* The White Seal *as it is sometimes called, is a beautiful song of mother love which forms the epigraph to the story of the same name in* The Jungle Book.

[Seal Lullaby]

Oh! hush thee, my baby, the night is behind us,
  And black are the waters that sparkled so green.
The moon, o'er the combers, looks downward to find us
  At rest in the hollows that rustle between.
Where billow meets billow, there soft by the pillow;
  Ah, weary wee flipperling, curl at thy ease!
The storm shall not wake thee, no shark shall overtake thee
  Asleep in the arms of the slow-swinging seas.

[1894]

The next poem is a most truthful – and harrowing - depiction of the complexities of love between man and woman. Kipling tells us that it was inspired by a friend of the barmaid at Gatti's music hall 'oo was mistook in 'er man.'[115]

Bertolt Brecht put some lines from this poem into the mouth of Polly Peachum in The Threepenny Opera.[116]

"Mary, Pity Women!"

You call yourself a man,
 For all you used to swear,
An' Leave me, as you can,
 My certain shame to bear?
 I 'ear! You do not care -
You done the worst you know.
 I 'ate you, grinnin' there ...
Ah, Gawd, I love you so!

Nice while it lasted, an' now it is over -
Tear out your 'eart an' good-bye to your lover!
What's the use o' grievin', when the mother that bore you
(Mary, pity women!) knew it all before you?

It aren't no false alarm,
 The finish to your fun;
You - you 'ave brung the 'arm,
 An' I'm the ruined one!
 An' now you'll off an' run
With some new fool in tow.
 Your 'eart? You 'aven't none ...
Ah, Gawd, I love you so!

---

115 *Something of Myself.*
116 Was nützt all dein Jammer/(Leih, Maria, dein Ohr mir!)/Wenn meine Mutter selber/Wusste all das vor mir.)

When a man is tired there is naught will bind 'im
All 'e solemn promised 'e will shove be'ind 'im.
What's the good o' prayin' for The Wrath to strike 'im
(Mary, pity women!), when the rest are like 'im?

What 'ope for me or - it?
 What's left for us to do?
I've walked with men a bit,
 But this -- but this is you.
 So 'elp me, Christ, it's true!
Where can I 'ide or go?
You coward through and through! ...
Ah, Gawd, I love you so!

All the more you give 'em the less are they for givin' -
Love lies dead, an' you cannot kiss 'im livin'.
Down the road 'e led you there is no returnin'
(Mary, pity women!), but you're late in learnin'!

You'd like to treat me fair?
 You can't, because we're pore?
We'd starve? What do I care!
 We might, but this is shore!
 I want the name - no more -
The name, an' lines to show,
 An' not to be an 'ore ...
Ah, Gawd, I love you so!

What the good o' pleadin', when the mother that bore you
(Mary, pity women!) knew it all before you?
Sleep on 'is promises an' wake to your sorrow
(Mary, pity women!), for we sail to-morrow.

[1896]

In The Ladies *a soldier reminisces about his various 'conquests', their diversity and their underlying similarity. Over-familiarity with the last two lines can tempt us to forget their fundamental egalitarianism.*

The Ladies

I've taken my fun where I've found it;
 I've rogued an' I've ranged in my time;
I've 'ad my pickin' o' sweethearts,
 An' four o' the lot was prime.
One was an 'arf-caste widow,
 One was a woman at Prome,
One was the wife of a *jemadar-sais*
 An' one is a girl at 'ome.

Now I aren't no 'and with the ladies,
 For, takin' 'em all along,
You never can say till you've tried 'em,
 An' then you are like to be wrong.
There's times when you'll think that you mightn't,
 There's times when you'll know that you might;
But the things you will learn from the Yellow an' Brown,
 They'll 'elp you a lot with the White!

I was a young 'un at 'Oogli,
 Shy as a girl to begin;
Aggie de Castrer she made me,
 An' Aggie was clever as sin;
Older than me, but my first 'un -
 More like a mother she were -
Showed me the way to promotion an' pay,
 An' I learned about women from 'er!

Then I was ordered to Burma,
 Actin' in charge o' Bazar,
An' I got me a tiddy live 'eathen
 Through buyin' supplies off 'er pa.

66

Funny an' yellow an' faithful -
Doll in a teacup she were -
But we lived on the square, like a true-married pair,
An' I learned about women from 'er!

Then we was shifted to Neemuch
(Or I might ha' been keepin' 'er now),
An' I took with a shiny she-devil,
 The wife of a nigger at Mhow;
'Taught me the gipsy-folks' *bolee;*
Kind o' volcano she were,
For she knifed me one night 'cause I wished she was white,
And I learned about women from 'er!

Then I come 'ome in a trooper,
 'Long of a kid o' sixteen -
Girl from a convent at Meerut,
 The straightest I ever 'ave seen.
Love at first sight was 'er trouble,
 She didn't know what it were;
An' I wouldn't do such, 'cause I liked 'er too much,
 But - I learned about women from 'er!

I've taken my fun where I've found it,
 An' now I must pay for my fun,
For the more you 'ave known o' the others
 The less will you settle to one;
An' the end of it's sittin' and thinking',
 An' dreamin' Hell-fires to see;
So be warned by my lot (which I know you will not),
 An' learn about women from me!

What did the Colonel's Lady think?
 Nobody never knew.
Somebody asked the Sergeant's Wife,
 An' she told 'em true!

When you get to a man in the case,
* They're like as a row of pins -*
For the Colonel's Lady an' Judy O'Grady
* Are sisters under their skins!*
[1896]

The Sergeant's Wedding *is a sketch of a relationship which everyone, except the two most involved, knows to be doomed to failure. Some critics have scorned the poem by reason of its having been written in the style of a music hall song: they should have concentrated on the substance.*

An echo of this poem can be found in the wedding song in Brecht's, Threepenny Opera.

The conventions of the day prevented use of words such as 'whore', which Kipling replaced here by 'etc.'

The Sergeant's Weddin'

'E was warned agin' 'er -
    That's what made 'im look;
She was warned agin' 'im -
    That is why she took.
'Wouldn't 'ear no reason,
    'Went an' done it blind;
We know all about 'em,
    They've got all to find!

Cheer for the Sergeant's weddin'—
    Give 'em one cheer more!
Grey gun-'orses in the lando,
    An' a rogue is married to etc..

What's the use o' tellin'
    'Arf the lot she's been?
'E's a bloomin' robber,
    An' 'e keeps canteen.
'Ow did 'e get 'is buggy?
    Gawd, you needn't ask!
'Made 'is forty gallon
    Out of every cask!

Watch 'im, with 'is 'air cut,
     Count us filin' by—
Won't the Colonel praise 'is
     Pop—u—lar—i—ty!
We 'ave scores to settle -
     Scores for more than beer;
She's the girl to pay 'em -
     That is why we're 'ere!

See the chaplain thinkin'?
     See the women smile?
Twig the married winkin'
     As they take the aisle?
Keep your side-arms quiet,
     Dressin' by the Band.
Ho! You 'oly beggars,
     Cough be'ind your 'and!

Now it's done an' over,
     'Ear the organ squeak,
"'Voice that breathed o'er Eden"—
     Ain't she got the cheek!
White an' laylock ribbons,
     Think yourself so fine!
I'd pray Gawd to take yer
     'Fore I made yer mine!

Escort to the kerridge,
     Wish 'im luck, the brute!
Chuck the slippers after—
     (Pity 'tain't a boot!)
Bowin' like a lady,
     Blushin' like a lad -
'Oo would say to see 'em
     Both is rotten bad?

Cheer for the Sergeant's weddin'-
Give 'em one cheer more!
Grey gun-'orses in the lando,
An' a rogue is married to, etc.

[1896]

Philip Burne-Jones,[117] *after being rejected as a suitor by the actress and so-cialite, Mrs Patrick Campbell, painted a picture of a woman sitting, some-what ambiguously, beside an insensible man, and asked his cousin, Kipling to write a song to accompany it, as what Andrew Lycett calls a 'promotional gimmick'. '[N]o one rated it high as poetry', wrote Charles Carrington, 'no one who had once heard it was likely to forget it. Prick it and blood would spurt.'*

Marghanita Laski suggested that the painting gave rise to our word, 'vamp', but the Oxford Dictionary of English Etymology (1966 edition) fails to con-firm this.

The Vampire

A fool there was and he made his prayer
(Even as you or I!)
To a rag and a bone and a hank of hair,
(We called her the woman who did not care),
But the fool he called her his lady fair—
(Even as you and I!)

Oh, the years we waste and the tears we waste,
And the work of our head and hand
Belong to the woman who did not know
(And now we know that she never could know)
And did not understand!

A fool there was and his goods he spent,
(Even as you and I!)
Honour and faith and a sure intent
(And it wasn't the least what the lady meant),
But a fool must follow his natural bent
(Even as you and I!)

---

117   Philip was the son of the more talented, Sir Edward Burne-Jones.

Oh, the toil we lost and the spoil we lost
And the excellent things we planned
Belong to the woman who didn't know why
(And now we know that she never knew why)
And did not understand!

The fool was stripped to his foolish hide,
(Even as you and I!)
Which she might have seen when she threw him aside -
(But it isn't on record the lady tried)
So some of him lived but the most of him died -
(Even as you and I!)

And it isn't the shame and it isn't the blame
That stings like a white-hot brand -
It's coming to know that she never knew why
(Seeing, at last, she could never know why)
And never could understand!

[1897]

There's little logical about love, but some relationships seem to be doomed to failure.

Although this memorable poem was written to accompany the story, 'In the Same Boat' Kipling claimed that it could stand alone 'without context'.[118] *It can be 'explained' by reference to the story, but, standing alone, it seems to be about inappropriate/mismatched love which, being acknowledged, is abandoned with relief.*

Or perhaps not.

'Helen All Alone'

In the same boat

There was darkness under Heaven
      For an hour's space -
Darkness that we knew was given
      Us for special grace.
Sun and moon and stars were hid,
      God had left His Throne,
When Helen came to me, she did,
      Helen all alone!

Side by side (because our fate
      Damned us ere our birth)
We stole out of Limbo Gate
      Looking for the Earth.
Hand in pulling hand amid
      Fear no dreams have known,
Helen ran with me, she did,
      Helen all alone!

When the Horror passing speech
      Hunted us along,

---

118 Pinney.

Each laid hold on each, and each
        Found the other strong.
In the teeth of Things forbid
        And Reason overthrown,
Helen stood by me, she did,
        Helen all alone!

When, at last, we heard those Fires
        Dull and die away,
When, at last, our linked desires
        Dragged us up to day;
When, at last, our souls were rid
        Of what that Night had shown,
Helen passed from me, she did,
        Helen all alone!

Let her go and find a mate,
        As I will find a bride,
Knowing naught of Limbo Gate
        Or Who are penned inside.
There is knowledge God forbid
        More than one should own.
So Helen went from me, she did,
Oh my soul, be glad she did!
Helen all alone!

[1917]

THE BURDEN OF EMPIRE

In Kipling's poem, *The Widow's Party* a private, asked what was the point of all his soldiering, replies professing ignorance, but in a way which answers the question.

> Ask my Colonel, for I don't know,
> Johnnie, my Johnnie, aha!
> We broke a King and we built a road -
> A court-house stands where the reg'ment goed.
> And the river's clean where the raw blood flowed
> When the Widow gives the party.

The Widow, of course, was Queen Victoria.

Wars, unavoidable or foolish, ending in victory or ignominy, seem to be a concomitant of empire; and not just the British empire.

ROME

It was all too tempting for the Victorians to see parallels between the British empire and the Roman. Historians tell us that such comparisons can be taken too far, but in Kipling's hands they invariably give cause for reflection.

In the first poem in this section the singer expresses his longing for Rome where dwells his faithless lover, Lalage. (The name meant chatterer in Greek.) A woman of that name is mentioned more than once in the Odes of Rome's great poet, Quintus Horatius Flaccus ('Horace'), of whose works Kipling was a lifelong admirer and imitator.[119]

Rimini is an ancient city on the Adriatic coast of Italy.

"Rimini"

(Marching Song of a Roman Legion of the Later Empire)

When I left Rome for Lalage's sake,
By the Legions' Road to Rimini,
She vowed her heart was mine to take
With me and my shield to Rimini -
(Till the Eagles flew from Rimini -)
And I've tramped Britain, and I've tramped Gaul
And the Pontic shore where the snow-flakes fall
As white as the neck of Lalage -
(As cold as the heart of Lalage!)
And I've lost Britain, and I've lost Gaul,
And I've lost Rome and, worst of all,
I've lost Lalage!

When you go by the Via Aurelia
As thousands have traveled before
Remember the Luck of the Soldier
Who never saw Rome any more!
Oh, dear was the sweetheart that kissed him,
And dear was the mother that bore;
But his shield was picked up in the heather,
And he never saw Rome any more!

---

119 The editors of Penguin's magnificent 'Horace in English' refer to Kipling as 'insufficiently recognised as one of our great Horation poets.'

And *he* left Rome, etc.

When you go by the Via Aurelia
That runs from the City to Gaul,
Remember the Luck of the Soldier
Who rose to be master of all!
He carried the sword and the buckler,
He mounted his guard on the Wall,
Till the Legions elected him Caesar,
And he rose to be master of all!

And *he* left Rome, etc.

It's twenty-five marches to Narbo,
It's forty-five more up the Rhone,
And the end may be death in the heather
Or life on an Emperor's throne.
But whether the Eagles obey us,
Or we go to the Ravens - alone,
I'd sooner be Lalage's lover
Than sit on an Emperor's throne!
We've *all* left Rome for Lalage's sake, etc.

[1906]

At first reading the next poem appears to be a celebration of empire; that is until the supposed date is spotted. It was the year the barbarians crossed the Rhine and ravaged Gaul. Four years later imperial Rome was sacked for the first time. It is a song of determined optimism which only the reader knows to be misplaced.

A British-Roman Song

(AD 406)

My father's father saw it not,
      And I, belike, shall never come
To look on that so-holy spot -
         The very Rome -

Crowned by all Time, all Art, all Might,
      The equal work of Gods and Man,
City beneath whose oldest height -
         The Race began!

Soon to send forth again a brood,
      Unshakable, we pray, that clings
To Rome's thrice-hammered hardihood -
         In arduous things.

Strong heart with triple armour bound,
      Beat strongly, for Thy life-blood runs,
Age after Age, the Empire round -
         In us thy Sons

Who, distant from the Seven Hills,
      Loving and serving much, require
Thee - thee to guard 'gainst home-born ills
         The Imperial Fire!

[1906]

The Pict Song *looks at Rome from underneath, as it were. It reminds one of the words of Tacitus, the great Roman historian who famously wrote of his own people, 'They ravage, they slaughter, they usurp, and they call it empire; they make a desert and they call it peace.'*

According to legend, the Picts, or 'painted people' resided in Caledonia and raided the Romans across Hadrian's wall. In fact, little is known about these enigmatic peoples.

It took an 'imperialist' like Kipling to put himself so realistically in the shoes of a subjected people.

A Pict Song

Rome never looks where she treads.
     Always her heavy hooves fall,
On our stomachs, our hearts or our heads;
     And Rome never heeds when we bawl.
Her sentries pass on - that is all,
     And we gather behind them in hordes,
And plot to reconquer the Wall,
     With only our tongues for our swords.

We are the Little Folk - we!
     Too little to love or to hate.
Leave us alone and you'll see
     How we can drag down the State!
We are the worm in the wood!
     We are the rot at the root!
We are the taint in the blood!
     We are the thorn in the foot!

Mistletoe killing an oak -
     Rats gnawing cables in two -
Moths making holes in a cloak -
     How they must love what they do!.

Yes - and *we* Little Folk too,
  We are busy as they -
Working our works out of view -
  Watch, and you'll see it some day!

No indeed! We are not strong,
  But we know Peoples that are.
Yes, and we'll guide them along,
  To smash and destroy you in War!
We shall be slaves just the same?
  Yes, we have always been slaves,
But you – you will die of the shame,
  And then we shall dance on your graves!

  We are the Little Folk! We! Etc.

[1906]

The next, most poignant, poem convincingly portrays the love a servant of the occupying power can come to feel for the conquered land, as Kipling well knew from his time in India.

No exact comparison can be made between ancient Roman and modern British military ranks, but at the time in which this poem was set a centurion in charge of a cohort might for literary purposes loosely be compared to a major. A legate was broadly equivalent to a general.

The Roman Centurion's Song

(Roman occupation of Britain, A.D. 300)

Legate, I had the news last night - my cohort ordered home
By ships to Portus Itius and thence by road to Rome.
I've marched the companies aboard, the arms are stowed below:
Now let another take my sword. Command me not to go!

I've served in Britain forty years, from Vectis to the Wall,
I have none other home than this, nor any life at all.
Last night I did not understand, but, now the hour draws near
That calls me to my native land, I feel that land is here.

Here where men say my name was made, here where my work was done;
Here where my dearest dead are laid - my wife - my wife and son;
Here where time, custom, grief and toil, age, memory, service, love,
Have rooted me in British soil. Ah, how can I remove?

For me this land, that sea, these airs, those folk and fields suffice.
What purple Southern pomp can match our changeful Northern skies,
Black with December snows unshed or pearled with August haze -
The clanging arch of steel-grey March, or June's long-lighted days?
You'll follow widening Rhodanus till vine and olive lean
Aslant before the sunny breeze that sweeps Nemausus clean
To Arelate's triple gate; but let me linger on,
Here where our stiff-necked British oaks confront Euroclydon!

You'll take the old Aurelian Road through shore-descending pines
Where, blue as any peacock's neck, the Tyrrhene Ocean shines.
You'll go where laurel crowns are won, but -will you e'er forget
The scent of hawthorn in the sun, or bracken in the wet?
Let me work here for Britain's sake - at any task you will -
A marsh to drain, a road to make or native troops to drill.
Some Western camp (I know the Pict) or granite Border keep,
Mid seas of heather derelict, where our old messmates sleep.

Legate, I come to you in tears - My cohort ordered home!
I've served in Britain forty years. What should I do in Rome?
Here is my heart, my soul, my mind - the only life I know.
I cannot leave it all behind. Command me not to go!

[1911]

The following lines describe the dying days of the 'doomed imperial [ie Roman] race' in terms that invite comparison with England's plight. They were inscribed by Kipling on the fly-leaf of a copy of Puck of Pook's Hill *which he gave to his friend, Sir Charles Oman. As well as being a military historian, Oman was a distinguished numismatist.*

The Coin Speaks

Singers sing for coin: but I,
Struck in Rome's last agony,
Shut the lips of Melody.

Many years my thin white face
Peered in every market-place
At the Doomed Imperial Race.

Warmed against and worn between
Hearts uncleansed and hands unclean -
What is there I have not seen?

Not an Empire dazed and old -
Smitten blind and stricken cold -
Bartering her sons for gold;

Not the Plebs her rulers please
From the public treasuries
With the bread and circuses

Not the hard-won fields restored,
At the egregious Senate's word,
To the savage and the Sword;

Not the People's God-like voice
As it welcomes or destroys
Month-old idols of its choice;

Not the Legions they disband,
Not the oarless ships unmanned,
Not the ruin of the land,
These I know and understand.

[1907]

INDIA

It is difficult now, when Britain is a mere offshore island of the European Union, to remember that within living memory it possessed the largest empire the world has known, covering almost a quarter of the earth's land surface. While the empire brought prosperity to 'the mother country' it also entailed extensive administrative and peace keeping responsibilities which were undertaken by a remarkably small cadre of officials and a tiny army, a few of whose members Kipling got to know well. But, as the poet soon learned, the price of empire was high.

In a letter to his cousin, Margaret Burne-Jones, he wrote, 'We spend our best men on the country like water and if ever a country was made better through 'the blood of martyrs' India is that country. I couldn't tell you now what the men one knows are doing but you can read for yourself if you will how Englishmen have laboured and died for the peoples of the country . . . have you ever heard of a 'demoralized district'; when tens of thousands of people are panic stricken say, with an invasion of cholera – or dying from famine? Do you know how Englishmen, Oxford men expensively educated, are turned off to 'do' that district – to make their own arrangements for the cholera camps; for the prevention of disorder; or for famine relief, to pull the business through or die – whichever God wills. Then another man, or maybe boy takes his place.'[120]

But Kipling didn't have his head in the clouds. He knew that the view from Windsor or Westminster was a world away from that from the peasant's hovel:

> Mogul Mahratta, and Mlech from the North,
> And White Queen over the Seas—

---

120 Quoted by David Gilmour.

God raiseth them up and driveth them forth
As the dust of the ploughshare flies in the breeze;
But the wheat and the cattle are all my care,
And the rest is the will of God.[121]

---

121 *What the People Said.*

The first poem in this section is a bitter-sweet mood piece which imagines a day in a traditional English Christmas, as celebrated by the British in India. It stresses how, amid all the festivities, the celebrants felt as distanced from India as from 'home'.

Christmas in India

Dim dawn behind the tamarisks - the sky is saffron-yellow -
    As the women in the village grind the corn,
And the parrots seek the riverside, each calling to his fellow
    That the Day, the staring Eastern Day, is born.
        Oh the white dust on the highway! Oh the stenches in the
    byway!
        Oh the clammy fog that hovers over earth!
    And at Home they're making merry 'neath the white and scarlet
berry -
        What part have India's exiles in their mirth?

Full day behind the tamarisks - the sky is blue and staring -
    As the cattle crawl afield beneath the yoke,
And they bear One o'er the field-path, who is past all hope or caring,
    To the ghat below the curling wreaths of smoke.
        Call on Rama, going slowly, as ye bear a brother lowly -
    Call on Rama - he may hear, perhaps, your voice!
    With our hymn-books and our psalters we appeal to other altars,
        And to-day we bid "good Christian men rejoice!"

High noon behind the tamarisks - the sun is hot above us -
    As at Home the Christmas Day is breaking wan.
They will drink our healths at dinner - those who tell us how they love us,
    And forget us till another year be gone!
        Oh the toil that knows no breaking! Oh the *Heimweh*, ceaseless,
    aching!
        Oh the black dividing Sea and alien Plain!
Youth was cheap - wherefore we sold it. Gold was good - we hoped to
hold it,
    And to-day we know the fulness of our gain.

Grey dusk behind the tamarisks - the parrots fly together -
　　　As the sun is sinking slowly over Home;
And his last ray seems to mock us shackled in a lifelong tether.
　　　That drags us back how'er so far we roam.
　　　　Hard her service, poor her payment - she in ancient, tattered raiment -
　　　　　　India, she the grim Stepmother of our kind.
　　　　　　If a year of life be lent her, if her temple's shrine we enter,
　　　The door is shut - we may not look behind.

Black night behind the tamarisks - the owls begin their chorus -
　　　As the conches from the temple scream and bray.
　With the fruitless years behind us, and the hopeless years before us,
　　　Let us honour, O my brother, Christmas Day!
　　　Call a truce, then, to our labours - let us feast with friends and neighbours,
And be merry as the custom of our caste;
For if "faint and forced the laughter," and if sadness follow after,
　　　We are richer by one mocking Christmas past.

(1886)

Kipling despised (it is not too strong a word) Members of Parliament and others who from a position of distant ignorance criticized the men responsible for protecting and administering Britain's vast empire. Pagett M.P. is a fantasy of revenge that many old India hands must have sympathized with. Not perhaps his best work, but memorable and true.

Pagett, M.P.

> *The toad beneath the harrow knows*
> *Exactly where each tooth-point goes.*
> *The butterfly upon the road*
> *Preaches contentment to that toad.*

Pagett, M.P., was a liar, and a fluent liar therewith, -
He spoke of the heat of India as "The Asian Solar Myth";
Came on a four months' visit, to "study the East," in November,
And I got him to sign an agreement vowing to stay till September.

March came in with the koil. Pagett was cool and gay,
Called me a "bloated Brahmin," talked of my "princely pay."
March went out with the roses. "Where is your heat?" said he.
"Coming," said I to Pagett, "Skittles!" said Pagett, M.P.

April began with the punkah, coolies, and prickly-heat, -
Pagett was dear to mosquitoes, sandflies found him a treat.
He grew speckled and mumpy-hammered, I grieve to say,
Aryan brothers who fanned him, in an illiberal way.

May set in with a dust-storm, - Pagett went down with the sun.
All the delights of the season tickled him one by one.
Imprimis - ten day's "liver" - due to his drinking beer;
Later, a dose of fever - slight, but he called it severe.

Dysent'ry touched him in June, after the Chota Bursat -
Lowered his portly person - made him yearn to depart.
He didn't call me a "Brahmin," or "bloated," or "overpaid,"
But seemed to think it a wonder that any one ever stayed.

July was a trifle unhealthy, - Pagett was ill with fear.
'Called it the "Cholera Morbus," hinted that life was dear.
He babbled of "Eastern exile," and mentioned his home with tears;
But I hadn't seen my children for close upon seven years.

We reached a hundred and twenty once in the Court at noon,
(I've mentioned Pagett was portly) Pagett, went off in a swoon.
That was an end to the business; Pagett, the perjured, fled
With a practical, working knowledge of "Solar Myths" in his head.

And I laughed as I drove from the station, but the mirth died out on my lips
As I thought of the fools like Pagett who write of their "Eastern trips,"
And the sneers of the travelled idiots who duly misgovern the land,
And I prayed to the Lord to deliver another one into my hand.

[1886]

The Love Song of Har Dyal *is in an unusual form for Kipling.* It *features in his story,* Beyond the Pale, *wherein the narrator claims that it 'is really pretty in the Vernacular'. No such song has yet been traced, so the claim may be no more than a storyteller's device.*

T.S. Eliot admitted to having based the title of his poem, The Love Song of J. Alfred Prufrock *on this.*

The Love Song of Har Dyal

Alone upon the housetops to the North
I turn and watch the lightning in the sky -
The glamour of thy footsteps in the North.
Come back to me, Beloved, or I die.

Below my feet the still bazar is laid -
Far, far below the weary camels lie -
The camels and the captives of thy raid.
Come back to me, Beloved, or I die.

My father's wife is old and harsh with years
And drudge of all my father's house am I -
My bread is sorrow and my drink is tears.
Come back to me, Beloved, or I die.

[1888]

Notwithstanding all the efforts of the imperial power, famine was an ever present threat to the indigenous population of the sub-continent. In 1887 Lord Dufferin, the Viceroy of India, was asked to conduct an inquiry into the condition of the people. His patrician conclusion was that 'over the greater part of India the condition of the lower classes of the agricultural population is not one which need cause any great anxiety at present'. Kipling disagreed.

He spoke for many with the following satire. It is in the form of a 'masque', a courtly entertainment in music and song. Angus Wilson described it as 'explosive'. The full version contains too many Hindu terms and references to long dead men to reproduce in full without extensive commentary: I trust that the following extracts convey the poem's essence.

The Masque of Plenty

[Extracts]

Argument - The Indian Government being minded to discover the economic condition of their lands, sent a Committee to inquire into it; and saw that it was good.

Scene - *The wooded heights of Simla.*
The Incarnation of the Government of India in the raiment
of the Angel of Plenty sings, to pianoforte accompaniment: -

"How sweet is the shepherd's sweet life!
    From the dawn to the even he strays -
He shall follow his sheep all the day
    And his tongue shall be filled with praise.
       (adagio dim.) Filled with praise!"

(largendo con sp.) Now this is the position,
    Go make an inquisition
    Into their real condition
    As swiftly as ye may.
    (p) Ay, paint our swarthy billions
    The richest of vermilions

Ere two well-led cotillions
   Have danced themselves away.
  ...

Interlude, *from Nowhere in Particular, to stringed and Oriental instruments.*
  Our cattle reel beneath the yoke they bear -
   The earth is iron and the skies are brass -
  And faint with fervour of the flaming air
   The languid hours pass.

  The well is dry beneath the village tree -
   The young wheat withers ere it reach a span,
  And belts of blinding sand show cruelly
   Where once the river ran.
  ...

Triumphal return to Simla of the Investigators, attired after
the manner of Dionysus, leading a pet tiger-cub in wreaths
of rhubarb-leaves, symbolical of India under medical treatment. They
sing:-
We have seen, we have written - behold it, the proof of our manifold toil!
In their hosts they assembled and told it - the tale of the Sons of the Soil.
We have said of the Sickness - "Where is it?" - and of Death - "It is far
from our ken," -
We have paid a particular visit to the affluent children of men.
We have trodden the mart and the well-curb - we have stooped to the
bield and the byre;
And the King may the forces of Hell curb for the People have all they
desire!
...

Recitative— *Government of India, with white satin wings*
and electro-plated harp:-
How beautiful upon the Mountains - in peace reclining,
Thus to be assured that our people are unanimously dining.
And though there are places not so blessed as others in natural
advantages, which, after all, was only to be expected,

Proud and glad are we to congratulate you upon the work
 you have thus ably effected.
(Cres.) How be-ewtiful upon the Mountains!

Hired Band, brasses only, full chorus: -
God bless the Squire
And all his rich relations
Who teach us poor people
      We eat our proper rations -
      We eat our proper rations,
      In spite of inundations,
      Malarial exhalations,
      And casual starvations,

We have, we have, they say we have -
We *have* our proper rations!
...

[1888]

As C.S. Lewis wrote, 'With a few exceptions imaginative literature in the eighteenth and nineteenth centuries had quietly omitted, or at least thrust into the background, the sort of thing which in fact occupies most of the waking hours of most men ... A whole range of strong sentiments and emotions- for many men the strongest of all – went with them. It was Kipling who first reclaimed for literature this enormous territory.'[122]

Talk of work and duty found its way into his stories and poems to an extent unequalled in the work of any other poet. It probably stemmed in part from his education at a school designed to prepare young men for the responsibilities of empire. Though he never became an official or a soldier, he got to know a wide range of such men well and drew from them the lesson, 'Save he serve, no man may rule'.[123]

As someone who suffered lengthy periods of ill health, Kipling learned that work can fulfill a yet deeper function:

> Heart may fail, and Strength outwear, and Purpose turn to Loathing,
> But the everyday affair of business, meals, and clothing,
> Builds a bulkhead 'twixt Despair and the Edge of Nothing. [124]

For Kipling, duty was closely allied with something he liked to call 'the law'. 'Keep ye the law - be swift in all obedience'[125], he wrote, '[n]ow this is the law of the jungle';[126] and so on. Mentioned often, he never defined his concept of law clearly. Outside its legal context his only attempt at definition was in *The Jungle Book*, wherein he wrote that, ' ... the strength

---

122 *Kipling's World*. Literature and Life. 1948
123 *A School Song*.
124 *The Supports*.
125 *A Song of the English*.
126 *The Law of the Wolves*.

of the Pack is the Wolf, and the strength of the Wolf is the Pack.'[127] Many theories have been offered as to Kipling's understanding of this concept, but the present editor doubts that he himself had a developed theory, so let me offer my own.

A curious feature of Kipling's works is their almost complete disregard of what, until 1947, was the most significant event in the history of the Raj, the mutiny of 1857 (or the First War of Independence, as it is now known by some in India)[128]. In a letter to a friend he wrote, "57 is the year we don't talk about and I know I can't'. This widespread rebellion by sepoys of the army of the East India Company was so unexpected, so widespread and so bloody, and the punishments meted out to the captured sepoys so brutal as to sear its memory into the collective consciousness of the British, yet it does not figure significantly in the works of Kipling, who was born only eight years after the event. Could the folk memory have manifested itself in the stress he placed upon duty and observance of 'the law'?

---

127 *The Wolf.*

128 His poem, *The Veterans* is a notable exception

This section begins with a light hearted portrayal of the joy of work.

When Earth's Last Picture is Painted

1892

When Earth's last picture is painted and the tubes are twisted and dried,
When the oldest colors have faded and the youngest critic has died,
We shall rest, and faith, we shall need it - lie down for an aeon or two,
'Till the Master of All Good Workmen shall put us to work anew!

And those that were good shall be happy: they shall sit in a golden chair;
They shall splash at a ten league canvas with brushes of comet's hair;
They shall find real saints to draw from - Magdalene, Peter, and Paul;
They'll work for an age at a sitting and never be tired at all!

And only the Master shall praise us, and only the Master shall blame.
And no one will work for the money and no one will work for fame.
But each for the joy of the working, and each, in his separate star,
Shall draw the Thing as he sees It for the God of Things as They are!

The next poem draws heavily on the Masonic tradition. Ultimately, the poet suggests, the only immortality we can hope for is recognition of our craft which builds on the work of our predecessors.

The Palace

1902

When I was a King and a Mason - a Master proven and skilled -
I cleared me ground for a Palace such as a King should build.
I decreed and dug down to my levels. Presently under the silt
I came on the wreck of a Palace such as a king had built.

There was no worth in the fashion - there was no wit in the plan -
Hither and thither, aimless, the ruined footings ran -
Masonry, brute, mishandled, but carven on every stone:
"After me cometh a Builder. Tell him I too have known."

Swift to my use in my trenches, where my well-planned ground-works grew,
I tumbled his quoins and his ashlars, and cut and reset them anew.
Lime I milled of his marbles; burned it slacked it, and spread;
Taking and leaving at pleasure the gifts of the humble dead.

Yet I despised not nor gloried; yet, as we wrenched them apart,
I read in the razed foundations the heart of that builder's heart.
As he had written and pleaded, so did I understand
The form of the dream he had followed in the face of the thing he had planned.
· · · · · · · · · ·

When I was a King and a Mason, in the open noon of my pride,
They sent me a Word from the Darkness. They whispered and called me aside.
They said - "The end is forbidden." They said - "Thy use is fulfilled.
Thy Palace shall stand as that other's - the spoil of a King who shall build."

100

I called my men from my trenches, my quarries my wharves and my sheers.
All I had wrought I abandoned to the faith of the faithless years.
Only I cut on the timber - only I carved on the stone:
"After me cometh a Builder. Tell him, I too have known."

The Sons of Martha *takes its text from one of the more domestic moments in the New Testament. It describes the occasion when Jesus was received in the house of two sisters, Martha and Mary. Martha felt obliged to lay on a meal for their guest, but Mary, who was seated at the feet of the teacher drinking in his words, disdained to help with the preparations. Martha complained, 'Lord, don't you care that my sister has left me to do the work by myself? Tell her to help me!' But Jesus would have none of it, saying, 'Martha, Martha, you are worried and upset about many things, but few things are needed—or indeed only one. Mary has chosen what is better, and it will not be taken away from her.' (Luke 10.38-42, NIV).*

In this poem the men whose labours keep society going are portrayed as 'the sons of Martha'. Kipling regarded it as one of the best things he had ever done.[129]

The Sons of Martha

1907

The sons of Mary seldom bother, for they have inherited that good part;
But the Sons of Martha favour their Mother of the careful soul and the troubled heart.
And because she lost her temper once, and because she was rude to the Lord her Guest,
Her Sons must wait upon Mary's Sons, world without end, reprieve, or rest.

It is their care in all the ages to take the buffet and cushion the shock.
It is their care that the gear engages; it is their care that the switches lock.
It is their care that the wheels run truly; it is their care to embark and entrain,
Tally, transport, and deliver duly the Sons of Mary by land and main.

They say to mountains, "Be ye removed." They say to the lesser floods, "Be dry."

---

129 Kipling's agent, quoted in Pinney.

Under their rods are the rocks reproved - they are not afraid of that which is high.
Then do the hill-tops shake to the summit - then is the bed of the deep laid bare,
That the Sons of Mary may overcome it, pleasantly sleeping and unaware.

They finger Death at their gloves' end where they piece and repiece the living wires.
He rears against the gates they tend: they feed him hungry behind their fires.
Early at dawn, ere men see clear, they stumble into his terrible stall,
And hale him forth a haltered steer, and goad and turn him till evenfall.

To these from birth is Belief forbidden; from these till death is Relief afar.
They are concerned with matters hidden - under the earthline their altars are-
The secret fountains to follow up, waters withdrawn to restore to the mouth,
And gather the floods as in a cup, and pour them again at a city's drouth.

They do not preach that their God will rouse them a little before the nuts work loose.
They do not teach that His Pity allows them to drop their job when they dam'-well choose.
As in the thronged and the lighted ways, so in the dark and the desert they stand,
Wary and watchful all their days that their brethren's day may be long in the land.

Raise ye the stone or cleave the wood to make a path more fair or flat -
Lo, it is black already with blood some Son of Martha spilled for that!
Not as a ladder from earth to Heaven, not as a witness to any creed,
But simple service simply given to his own kind in their common need.

And the Sons of Mary smile and are blessèd – they know the Angels are on their side.
They know in them is the Grace confessèd, and for them are the Mercies multiplied.

They sit at the Feet - they hear the Word - they see how truly the Promise runs.
They have cast their burden upon the Lord, and – the Lord He lays it on Martha's Sons!

The next, deceptively simple, poem is sometimes read – and sold in garden nurseries - at face value, as if it had come from the pen of Alan Titchmarsh. It is probably Kipling's clearest statement of the central role of work in a man's life.

The Glory of the Garden

Our England is a garden that is full of stately views,
Of borders, beds and shrubberies and lawns and avenues,
With statues on the terraces and peacocks strutting by;
But the Glory of the Garden lies in more than meets the eye.

For where the old thick laurels grow, along the thin red wall,
You'll find the tool- and potting-sheds which are the heart of all
The cold-frames and the hot-houses, the dung-pits and the tanks,
The rollers, carts, and drain-pipes, with the barrows and the planks.

And there you'll see the gardeners, the men and 'prentice boys
Told off to do as they are bid and do it without noise ;
For, except when seeds are planted and we shout to scare the birds,
The Glory of the Garden it abideth not in words.

And some can pot begonias and some can bud a rose,
And some are hardly fit to trust with anything that grows ;
But they can roll and trim the lawns and sift the sand and loam,
For the Glory of the Garden occupieth all who come.

Our England is a garden, and such gardens are not made
By singing:-" Oh, how beautiful," and sitting in the shade
While better men than we go out and start their working lives
At grubbing weeds from gravel-paths with broken dinner-knives.

There's not a pair of legs so thin, there's not a head so thick,
There's not a hand so weak and white, nor yet a heart so sick
But it can find some needful job that's crying to be done,
For the Glory of the Garden glorifieth every one.

Then seek your job with thankfulness and work till further orders,
If it's only netting strawberries or killing slugs on borders;
And when your back stops aching and your hands begin to harden,
You will find yourself a partner In the Glory of the Garden.

Oh, Adam was a gardener, and God who made him sees
That half a proper gardener's work is done upon his knees,
So when your work is finished, you can wash your hands and pray
For the Glory of the Garden that it may not pass away!
And the Glory of the Garden it shall never pass away !

[1911]

WAR AND THE SOLDIER

No one has portrayed the life of the solder, in barracks or in the field, as realistically and movingly as Kipling. His descriptions of battle are unequalled despite the fact that he himself was only once under fire, and that in a minor way.

A SOLDIER'S LIFE

Kipling first made acquaintance with 'the brutal soldiery' in Lahore, where he,

> 'came to realise the bare horrors of the private's life, and the unnecessary torments he endured on account of the Christian doctrine which lays down that 'the wages of sin is death.' It was counted impious that bazaar prostitutes should be inspected; or that the men should be taught elementary precautions in their dealings with them. This official virtue cost our Army in India nine thousand expensive white men a year always laid up from venereal disease... Heaven knows the men died fast enough from typhoid, which seemed to have something to do with water, but we were not sure; or from cholera, which was manifestly a breath of the Devil that could kill all on one side of a barrack-room and spare the others; from seasonal fever; or from what was described as 'blood-poisoning.'[130]

---

130 *Something of Myself.*

The first poem in this section was not rated highly by its author, and its merits are sometimes overlooked.

The Story of Tommy is a young man's poem which showed signs of future promise, for example in its repetition of the significant phrase, 'Tommy, aged twenty' and the interposition at a critical moment of the incongruous, 'Late night owls are chuckling.' Notwithstanding the subtitle, the poem exemplifies how small human weaknesses can build up into tragedy. Drowsiness caused the coolie to fall asleep on duty; drowsiness and drink caused Tommy to believe that discharging his rifle was just a jape. The result was a double tragedy which the authorities could not afford to overlook.

At the heart of the poem is compassion, the theme that was to run through almost all Kipling's serious verse, even a trifle like this written by a young man of only nineteen Summers.

The Story of Tommy

A Story without A Moral

This is the story of Tommy, aged twenty and drunk in his cot;
Marvellous drunk was Tommy, and the night was marvellous hot;
And the fever had held him all day, till Tommy was told by his 'chum'
That the worst of fevers would yield to a couple of 'goes' of rum.–
So he drank till the bare plain rocked 'neath his regulation boots,
And kept the liquor in place with a dozen *bazar* cheroots.

Marvellous hot was the night (hot as they make 'em in June),
Merrily came the mosquito and cheered his soul with a tune,
Over the nose of Tommy softly the punkah swept.

But coolies are only human, and somehow that coolie slept.–
Sweating and swearing profusely, dizzy and dazed with his smoke –
Mad with the drink and the fever, Tommy, aged twenty, awoke.

"Zor se kencho you soor!" Never an answering wrench,
Peacefully slumbered the coolie, *"Kencho you budzard, kench!"*
Three times Tommy had called him; gaily he slumbered on.
In at the barrack-room windows softly the moonbeams shone.
Gleamed on a polished belt-jag - gleamed on a barrel brown,
Stuck in a rack, and inviting Tommy to take 'em down.

Only an arm's length away, swaddled in paper and twine
Ten regulation "pickets" - if you subtract one, nine.
Tommy has settled that question as "Little Jack Horner" of yore,
Clutches the smooth brown barrel, staggers across the floor.
Only a tug at the lever, only a jerk of the thumb,
Now for the last temptation. Query. Will Tommy succumb?

Mistily muses Tommy - finger laid on the trigger:–
Ain't it a bloomin' lark to frighten a blasted nigger?"
Now fur to wake up the *soor!"* Never a sign from the coolie.
Tommy has shouldered the rifle - strives to present it duly.
Little night-owls are chuckling. Loudly the coolie respires,
Laughing aloud as he does so, Tommy, aged twenty, fires.

Merrily hiccupped Tommy, when they locked him up in the dark.
Tried to explain to the Guard how it was only a "lark."
Didn't remember at trial aught that he did or said,
Wherefore was justly ordained to be "hanged by the neck till dead."
Waited a couple of weeks, while the *padris* came and harangued,
Then, in the Central Jail, Tommy aged twenty, was hanged.

[1884]

There is a legend that Queen Victoria was annoyed by the references to herself in the following poem, but there is no evidence to support it.

The poem has sometimes been read as an imperialist boast; in fact it is a soldier's reminder that empire is bought and kept at the cost of men's lives.

The Widow at Windsor

'Ave you 'eard o' the Widow at Windsor
    With a hairy gold crown on 'er 'ead?
She 'as ships on the foam - she 'as millions at 'ome,
    An' she pays us poor beggars in red.
        (Ow, poor beggars in red!)
There's 'er nick on the cavalry 'orses,
    There's 'er mark on the medical stores -
An' 'er troopers you'll find with a fair wind be'ind
    That takes us to various wars.
        (Poor beggars! - barbarious wars!)
           Then 'ere's to the Widow at Windsor,
                An' 'ere's to the stores an' the guns,
            The men an' the 'orses what makes up the forces
            O' Missis Victorier's sons.
        (Poor beggars! Victorier's sons!)

Walk wide o' the Widow at Windsor,
    For 'alf o' Creation she owns:
We 'ave bought 'er the same with the sword an' the flame,
    An' we've salted it down with our bones.
        (Poor beggars! - it's blue with our bones!)
Hands off o' the sons o' the Widow,
    Hands off o' the goods in 'er shop,
For the Kings must come down an' the Emperors frown
    When the Widow at Windsor says "Stop"!
        (Poor beggars! - we're sent to say "Stop"!)
           Then 'ere's to the Lodge o' the Widow,

From the Pole to the Tropics it runs -
       To the Lodge that we tile with the rank an' the file,
          An' open in form with the guns.
          (Poor beggars! - it's always they guns!)

We 'ave 'eard o' the Widow at Windsor,
          It's safest to let 'er alone:
For 'er sentries we stand by the sea an' the land
          Wherever the bugles are blown.
                    (Poor beggars! - an' don't we get blown!)
Take 'old o' the Wings o' the Mornin',
          An' flop round the earth till you're dead;
But you won't get away from the tune that they play
          To the bloomin' old rag over'ead.
(Poor beggars! - it's 'ot over'ead!)
          Then 'ere's to the sons o' the Widow,
                    Wherever, 'owever they roam.
'Ere's all they desire, an' if they require
          A speedy return to their 'ome.
(Poor beggars! - they'll never see 'ome!)

[1892]

Comradeship between men who have shared great dangers and hardships together can be 'passin' the love o' women'.

Hilaire Belloc selected the next poem as one of Kipling's two best. The chorus is said to be based on The Dead March from Saul.

"Follow Me 'ome"

There was no one like him, 'Orse or Foot,
     Nor any o' the Guns I knew;
An' because it was so, why, o' course 'e went and died,
     Which is just what the best men do.

So it's knock out your pipes an' follow me!
And it's finish up your swipes an' follow me!
     Oh, 'ark to the big drum calling,
         Follow me - follow me 'ome!

'Is mare she neighs the 'ole day long,
     She paws the 'ole night through,
An' she won't take 'er feed 'cause o' waitin' for 'is step,
     Which is just what a beast would do.

'Is girl she goes with a bombardier
     Before 'er month is through;
An' the banns are up in church, for she's got the beggar hooked,
     Which is just what a girl would do.

We fought 'bout a dog - last week it was -
     No more than a round or two;
But I strook 'im cruel 'ard, and I wish I 'adn't now,
     Which is just what a man can't do.

'E was all that I 'ad in the way of a friend,
     And I've 'ad to find one new;

But I'd give my pay an' stripe for to get the beggar back,
    Which it's just too late to do!

So it's knock out your pipes an' follow me!
And it's finish up your swipes an' follow me!
    Oh, 'ark to the fifes a-crawlin!
        Follow me - follow me home!

Take 'im away! E's gone where the best men go.
 Take 'im away! An' the gun-wheels turning slow.
 Take 'im away! There's more from the place 'e came.
Take 'im away, with the limber and the drum.

For it's "Three rounds blank" and follow me,
An' it's "Thirteen rank" an' follow me;
    Oh, passin' the love o' women,
        Follow me - follow me 'ome!

[1894]

'Birds of Prey' is a finely observed description of troops embarking for foreign service. Carrington called it a 'savagely cynical-sentimental song' in which "Knocked 'em in the Old Kent Road" drifts in and out of the rhythm'.

'Birds of Prey' March

(Troops for Foreign Service)

March! The mud is cakin' good about our trousies.
      Front! - eyes front, an' watch the Colour-casin's drip.
Front! The faces of the women in the 'ouses
      Ain't the kind o' things to take aboard the ship.

Cheer! An' we'll never march to victory.
Cheer! An' we'll never live to 'ear the canon roar!
      The Large Birds o' Prey
      They will carry us away,
An' you'll never see your soldiers any more!

Wheel! Oh, keep your touch; we're goin' round a corner.
      Time! - mark time, an' let the men be'ind us close.
Lord! the transport's full, an' 'alf our lot not on 'er -
      Cheer, O cheer! We're going off where no one knows.

March! The Devil's none so black as 'e is painted!
      Cheer! We'll 'ave some fun before we're put away.
'Alt, an' 'and 'er out - a woman's gone and fainted!
      Cheer! Get on - Gawd 'elp the married men to-day!

Hoi! Come up, you 'ungry beggars, to yer sorrow.
      ('Ear them say they want their tea, an' want it quick!)
You won't have no mind for slingers, not to-morrow -
      No; you'll put the 'tween-decks stove out, bein' sick!

'Alt! The married kit 'as all to go before us!
      'Course it's blocked the bloomin' gangway up again!

Cheer, O cheer the 'Orse Guards watchin' tender o'er us,
  Keepin' us since eight this mornin' in the rain!

Stuck in 'eavy marchin'-order, sopped and wringin' -
  Sick, before our time to watch 'er 'eave an' fall,
'Ere's your 'appy 'ome at last, an' stop your singin'.
  'Alt! Fall in along the troop-deck! Silence all!

Cheer! For we'll never live to see no bloomin' victory!
Cheer! An' we'll never live to 'ear the cannon roar!
    (One cheer more!)
        The jackal an' the kite
        'Ave an 'ealthy appetite,

An' you'll never see your soldiers any more! ('Ip! Urroar!)
        The eagle an' the crow
        They are waitin' ever so,
An' you'll never see your soldiers any more! ('Ip! Urroar!)
        Yes, the Large Birds o' Prey
        They will carry us away,
An' you'll never see your soldiers any more!

[1895]

It is a truism that the life of a soldier is one of boredom, enlivened by brief flashes of horror. During the Boer War the railway was a vital supply line for the British through the Karoo, a semi-desert region of South Africa. This unforgettably poem describes the majestic African countryside seen through the eyes of the bored soldiers in a block house guarding the bridge 'Not combatants', they observe ruefully, 'only details guarding the line'.

More than in other poems, 'Bridge Guard' evokes its atmosphere through colours, and at night sound; the sound of a whistle, the Hottentot herders and contracting steel. But, then, there is little to see at night.

Bridge-guard in the Karoo

1901

"...and will supply details to guard the Blood River Bridge"
District Orders: Lines of Communication - South African War.

Sudden the desert changes,
  The raw glare softens and clings,
Till the aching Oudtshoorn ranges
  Stand up like the thrones of Kings -

Ramparts of slaughter and peril -
  Blazing, amazing, aglow -
'Twixt the sky-line's belting beryl
  And the wine-dark flats below.

Royal the pageant closes,
  Lit by the last of the sun -
Opal and ash-of-roses,
  Cinnamon, umber, and dun.

The twilight swallows the thicket,
  The starlight reveals the ridge.
The whistle shrills to the picket -
  We are changing guard on the bridge.

(Few, forgotten and lonely,
        Where the empty metals shine -
No, not combatants - only
        Details guarding the line.)

We slip through the broken panel
        Of fence by the ganger's shed;
We drop to the waterless channel
        And the lean track overhead;

We stumble on refuse of rations,
        The beef and the biscuit-tins;
We take our appointed stations,
        And the endless night begins.

We hear the Hottentot herders
        As the sheep click past to the fold -
And the click of the restless girders
        As the steel contracts in the cold -

Voices of jackals calling
        And, loud in the hush between,
A morsel of dry earth falling
        From the flanks of the scarred ravine.

And the solemn firmament marches,
        And the hosts of heaven rise
Framed through the iron arches—
        Banded and barred by the ties,

Till we feel the far track humming,
        And we see her headlight plain,
And we gather and wait her coming -
        The wonderful north-bound train.

(Few, forgotten and lonely,
        Where the white car-windows shine -
No, not combatants - only
        Details guarding the line.)

Quick, ere the gift escape us!
        Out of the darkness we reach
For a handful of week-old papers
        And a mouthful of human speech.

And the monstrous heaven rejoices,
        And the earth allows again,
Meetings, greetings, and voices
        Of women talking with men.

So we return to our places,
        As out on the bridge she rolls;
And the darkness covers our faces,
        And the darkness re-enters our souls.

More than a little lonely
        Where the lessening tail-lights shine.
No - not combatants - only
        Details guarding the line!

Who other than Kipling has written a poem about the experience of being a prisoner of war guard? Half-Ballade of Waterval, *set in the camp in which the Boers kept most of their English prisoners, is a telling lesson in humility.*

Half-Ballade of Waterval

(Non-Commissioned Officers in Charge of Prisoners)

When by the labour of my 'ands
     I've 'elped to pack a transport tight
With prisoners for foreign lands,
     I ain't transported with delight.
     I know it's only just an' right,
     But yet it somehow sickens me,
For I 'ave learned at Waterval
     The meanin' of captivity.

Be'ind the pegged barb-wire strands,
     Beneath the tall electric light,
We used to walk in bare-'ead bands,
     Explainin' 'ow we lost our fight;
An' that is what they'll do to-night
     Upon the steamer out at sea,
If I 'ave learned at Waterval
     The meanin' of captivity.

They'll never know the shame that brands -
     Black shame no livin' down makes white -
The mockin' from the sentry-stands,
     The women's laugh, the gaoler's spite.
     We are too bloomin'-much polite,
     But that is 'ow I'd 'ave us be . ...
Since I 'ave learned at Waterval
     The meanin' of captivity.

They'll get those draggin' days all right,
     Spent as a foreigner commands,

An' 'orrors of the locked-up night,
　　　　With 'Ell's own thinkin' on their 'ands.
　　　　I'd give the gold o' twenty Rands
　　　　　　(If it was mine) to set 'em free
For I 'ave learned at Waterval
　　　　The meanin' of captivity!

[1903]

During Kipling's lifetime, Britain experienced a number of imperial conflicts of ever increasing magnitude, including the second and third Anglo-Afghan wars.

His own experience of the North West frontier was limited. In 1885, while covering a state visit, his party stopped at the frontier outpost of Fort Jumrood, where the young journalist wandered off by himself into the Khyber Pass. Many years later he wrote, 'I was shot at, but without malice, by a rapparee[131] who disapproved of his ruler's foreign policy...'[132]

He could not have anticipated that, a century later, British soldiers would be dying in yet a fourth Afghan war. As with all our interventions in this region the British found it impossible wholly to overcome a primitive (by our standards) people whose abilities and courage their leaders consistently under-estimated.

---

131 Bandit.
132 *Something of Myself.*

Death comes - and I use the present tense deliberately - all too easily to the young British officer in the area once known as the North West Frontier. Though not particularly profound, Arithmetic on the Frontier *is an amazing accomplishment for someone who had barely reached his majority. The reader might spare a moment to ponder how little the soldier's lot has improved since his day.*

Arithmetic on the Frontier

A great and glorious thing it is
       To learn, for seven years or so,
The Lord knows what of that and this,
       Ere reckoned fit to face the foe -
The flying bullet down the Pass,
That whistles clear: "All flesh is grass."

Three hundred pounds per annum spent
       On making brain and body meeter
For all the murderous intent
       Comprised in "villainous saltpetre".
And after?- Ask the Yusufzaies
What comes of all our 'ologies.

A scrimmage in a Border Station -
       A canter down some dark defile
Two thousand pounds of education
       Drops to a ten-rupee *jezail* -
The Crammer's boast, the Squadron's pride,
Shot like a rabbit in a ride!

No proposition Euclid wrote
       No formulae the text-books know,
Will turn the bullet from your coat,
       Or ward the tulwar's downward blow.
Strike hard who cares - shoot straight who can
The odds are on the cheaper man.

One sword-knot stolen from the camp
        Will pay for all the school expenses
Of any Kurrum Valley scamp
        Who knows no word of moods and tenses,
But, being blessed with perfect sight,
Picks off our messmates left and right.

With home-bred hordes the hillsides teem.
        The troopships bring us one by one,
At vast expense of time and steam,
        To slay Afridis where they run.
The "captives of our bow and spear"
Are cheap, alas! as we are dear.

[1886]

Death does not always come at the hands of the enemy. The movingly sad Ford o' Kabul River *is based upon an incident in the second Afghan war in which forty six men of the 10th Hussars were swept away and died in the icy waters of Kabul river. (The poem seems to suggest that the ford was in Kabul town. In fact, it was 70 miles east.)*

"Ford o' Kabul River"

Kabul town's by Kabul river -
    Blow the bugle, draw the sword -
There I lef' my mate for ever,
      Wet an' drippin' by the ford.
          Ford, ford, ford o' Kabul river,
             Ford o' Kabul river in the dark !
There's the river up and brimmin', an' there's 'arf a squadron swimmin'
      'Cross the ford o' Kabul river in the dark.

Kabul town's a blasted place -
    Blow the bugle, draw the sword -
'Strewth I sha'n't forget 'is face
      Wet an' drippin' by the ford !
          Ford, ford, ford o' Kabul river,
             Ford o' Kabul river in the dark !
     Keep the crossing-stakes beside you, an' they will surely guide
you
      'Cross the ford o' Kabul river in the dark.

Kabul town is sun and dust -
    Blow the bugle, draw the sword -
I'd ha' sooner drowned fust
      'Stead of 'im beside the ford.
          Ford, ford, ford o' Kabul river,
             Ford o' Kabul river in the dark !
     You can 'ear the 'orses threshin', you can 'ear the men a-splashin',
      'Cross the ford o' Kabul river in the dark.

Kabul town was ours to take -
    Blow the bugle, draw the sword -
I'd ha' left it for 'is sake -
    'Im that left me by the ford.
        Ford, ford, ford o' Kabul river,
            Ford o' Kabul river in the dark!
      It's none so bloomin' dry there; ain't you never comin' nigh there,
        'Cross the ford o' Kabul river in the dark ?

Kabul town'll go to Hell -
    Blow the bugle, draw the sword -
'Fore I see him 'live an' well -
    'Im the best beside the ford.
        Ford, ford, ford o' Kabul river,
            Ford o' Kabul river in the dark !
      Gawd 'elp 'em if they blunder, for their boots'll pull 'em under,
      By the ford o' Kabul river in the dark.

Turn your 'orse from Kabul town -
    Blow the bugle, draw the sword -
'Im an' 'arf my troop is down,
    Down an' drownded by the ford.
        Ford, ford, ford o' Kabul river,
            Ford o' Kabul river in the dark !
      There's the river low an' fallin', but it ain't no use o' callin'
        'Cross the ford o' Kabul river in the dark.

[1890]

In The Young British Soldier *a drill sergeant gives the new recruits a glimpse of what is in store for them in Afghanistan.*

Even now, pastiches of this poem written by squaddies are circulating on the internet. Their rough-hewn prosody may be inferior to Kipling's, but the strength and nature of their sentiments (inadequate weapons and equipment, poor strategy and ill thought-out objectives) demonstrate how little the plight of 'the young British soldier' has changed since the poet's day.

The Young British Soldier

When the 'arf-made recruity goes out to the East
'E acts like a babe an' 'e drinks like a beast,
An' 'e wonders because 'e is frequent deceased
  Ere 'e's fit for to serve as a soldier.
    Serve, serve, serve as a soldier,
    Serve, serve, serve as a soldier,
    Serve, serve, serve as a soldier,
      So-oldier *of* the Queen!

Now all you recruities what's drafted to-day,
You shut up your rag-box an' 'ark to my lay,
An' I'll sing you a soldier as far as I may:
  A soldier what's fit for a soldier.
    Fit, fit, fit for a soldier . . .

First mind you steer clear o' the grog-sellers' huts,
For they sell you Fixed Bay'nets that rots out your guts -
Ay, drink that 'ud eat the live steel from your butts -
  An' it's bad for the young British soldier.
    Bad, bad, bad for the soldier ...

When the cholera comes - as it will past a doubt -
Keep out of the wet and don't go on the shout,

For the sickness gets in as the liquor dies out,
      An' it crumples the young British soldier.
            Crum-, crum-, crumples the soldier ...

But the worst o' your foes is the sun over'ead:
You must wear your 'elmet for all that is said:
If 'e finds you uncovered 'e'll knock you down dead,
      An' you'll die like a fool of a soldier.
          Fool, fool, fool of a soldier ...

If you're cast for fatigue by a sergeant unkind,
Don't grouse like a woman nor crack on nor blind;
Be handy and civil, and then you will find
      That it's beer for the young British soldier.
      Beer, beer, beer for the soldier ...

Now, if you must marry, take care she is old -
A troop-sergeant's widow's the nicest I'm told,
For beauty won't help if your rations is cold,
      Nor love ain't enough for a soldier.
         Nough, 'nough, 'nough for a soldier ...

If the wife should go wrong with a comrade, be loath
To shoot when you catch 'em - you'll swing, on my oath! -
Make 'im take 'er and keep 'er: that's Hell for them both,
      An' you're shut o' the curse of a soldier.
        Curse, curse, curse of a soldier ...

When first under fire an' you're wishful to duck,
Don't look nor take 'eed at the man that is struck,
Be thankful you're livin', and trust to your luck
      And march to your front like a soldier.
        Front, front, front like a soldier ...

When 'arf of your bullets fly wide in the ditch,
Don't call your Martini a cross-eyed old bitch;
She's human as you are - you treat her as sich,
      An' she'll fight for the young British soldier.
          Fight, fight, fight for the soldier ...

When shakin' their bustles like ladies so fine,
The guns o' the enemy wheel into line,
Shoot low at the limbers an' don't mind the shine,
      For noise never startles the soldier.
          Start-, start-, startles the soldier ...

If your officer's dead and the sergeants look white,
Remember it's ruin to run from a fight:
So take open order, lie down, and sit tight,
      An' wait for supports like a soldier.
          Wait, wait, wait like a soldier ...

When you're wounded and left on Afghanistan's plains,
An' the women come out to cut up what remains,
Jest roll to your rifle and blow out your brains
      An' go to your Gawd like a soldier.
          Go, go, go like a soldier,
          Go, go, go like a soldier,
          Go, go, go like a soldier,
          So-oldier of the Queen!

[1890]

The 27 July 1880 was a black day for the British army. Two brigades of British and Indian soldiers were defeated at Maiwand pass by an Afghan force, with the loss of over a thousand men. The British were outnumbered and could not compete with the Afghan's breech-loading and rifled artillery or their superior Martini-Henry rifle. Before their destruction, the 66th regiment of foot, the Berkshires, fought with outstanding bravery, but a small number of them broke on the field of battle, as dramatized in the following poem.

Maiwand is in the Afghan province of Kandahar, from which at the time of writing British troops are being withdrawn after yet another ineffective attempt to 'pacify' the Afghans.

That Day

It got beyond all orders an' it got beyond all 'ope;
     It got to shammin' wounded an' retirin' from the 'alt.
'Ole companies was lookin' for the nearest road to slope;
     It were just a bloomin' knock-out - an' our fault!

Now there ain't no chorus 'ere to give,
     Nor there ain't no band to play;
An' I wish I was dead 'fore I done what I did,
     Or seen what I seed that day!

We was sick o' bein' punished, an' we let 'em know it, too;
     An' a company-commander up an' 'it us with a sword,
An' some one shouted "'Ook it!" an' it come to sove-ki-poo,
     An' we chucked our rifles from us - O my Gawd!

There was thirty dead an' wounded on the ground we wouldn't keep -
     No, there wasn't more than twenty when the front begun to go;
But, Christ! along the line o' flight they cut us up like sheep,
     An' that was all we gained by doin' so.

I 'eard the knives be'ind me, but I dursn't face my man,

Nor I don't know where I went to, 'cause I didn't 'alt to see,
Till I 'eard a beggar squealin' out for quarter as 'e ran,
    An' I thought I knew the voice an' - it was me!

We was 'idin' under bedsteads more than 'arf a march away;
    We was lyin' up like rabbits all about the countryside;
An' the major cursed 'is Maker 'cause 'e lived to see that day,
An' the colonel broke 'is sword acrost, an' cried.

We was rotten 'fore we started - we was never disciplined;
    We made it out a favour if an order was obeyed;
Yes, every little drummer 'ad 'is rights an' wrongs to mind,
    So we had to pay for teachin' - an' we paid!

The papers 'id it 'andsome, but you know the Army knows;
    We was put to groomin' camels till the regiments withdrew,
An' they gave us each a medal for subduin' England's foes,
    An' I 'ope you like my song - because it's true!

An' there ain't no chorus 'ere to give,
    Nor there ain't no band to play;
But I wish I was dead 'fore I done what I did,
    Or seen what I seed that day!

[1895]

130

While Kipling is not generally thought of as being among the great flowering of poetry which occurred during and after the '14-'18 war, he can lay claim to being one of the country's foremost poets of war. His poems were not in the 'gung ho' style of earlier combats, but the more thoughtful and sad contemplation of the effects of industrialized warfare.

As well as having lived through a number of imperial wars Kipling also had the ability to look back to the wars of earlier days.

The inconclusive battle of Edgehill in Warwickshire, on 23 October 1642,
was the first significant military confrontation in the war between England's
King and Parliament. It was a struggle which was to continue in one form or
another for the next nine years. As Kipling points out in this, his only poem
on the English Civil War, there are few conflicts so bitter as those between
brother and brother.

Edgehill fight

(Civil wars, 1642)

Naked and grey the Cotswolds stand
    Beneath the autumn sun,
And the stubble-fields on either hand
    Where Stour and Avon run.
There is no change in the patient land
    That has bred us every one.

She should have passed in cloud and fire
    And saved us from this sin
Of war - red war - 'twixt child and sire,
    Household and kith and kin,
In the heart of a sleepy Midland shire,
    With the harvest scarcely in.

But there is no change as we meet at last
    On the brow-head or the plain,
And the raw astonished ranks stand fast
    To slay or to be slain
By the men they knew in the kindly past
    That shall never come again -

By the men they met at dance or chase,
    In the tavern or the hall,

At the justice-bench and the market-place,
    At the cudgel-play or brawl -
Of their own blood and speech and race,
    Comrades or neighbours all!

More bitter than death this day must prove
    Whichever way it go,
For the brothers of the maids we love
    Make ready to lay low
Their sisters sweethearts, as we move
    Against our dearest foe.

Thank Heaven! At last the trumpets peal
    Before our strength gives way.
For King or for the Commonweal -
    No matter which they say,
The first dry rattle of new-drawn steel
    Changes the world to-day!

[1911]

There is a widespread misconception that the subject of the next poem is Kipling's son, John. But John was never called Jack in the family, and the poem clearly refers to a sailor (known generically as Jack Tar), who died at the great naval battle of Jutland. The most likely candidate is Boy (1st Class) John Travers Cornwell VC of the "Chester', who was feted by the Press in 1916, just before this poem was published.

Nevertheless, in writing these lines barely a twelvemonth after his son's death, Kipling could not have been unmindful of his own pain.

Prof. Dobrée judged that this poem alone might establish Kipling's right to a high place among 'romantic' poets. Of almost equal worth is his less well known piece, the pathetic, A Nativity (not included in this anthology).

"My Boy Jack"

(1914 – 18)

'Ave you news of my boy Jack?"
     Not this tide.
"When d'you think that he'll come back?"
     Not with this wind blowing, and this tide.

"Has any one else had word of him?"
     Not this tide.
For what is sunk will hardly swim,
     Not with this wind blowing, and this tide.

"Oh, dear, what comfort can I find?"
     None this tide,
     Nor any tide,
Except he did not shame his kind -
     Not even with that wind blowing, and that tide.

Then hold your head up all the more,
　　　This tide,
　　　And every tide;
Because he was the son you bore,
　　　And gave to that wind blowing and that tide.

[1916]

It is tempting to think of the Great War as having taken place exclusively in and around Belgium, the so called cockpit of Europe, but in fact the battlefields stretched well beyond, even as far as Africa and the Middle East. It was in the region then known as Mesopotamia (now Iraq) that the British suffered one of their most humiliating defeats. The consequences for those involved were appalling.

In 1917, a British Indian Division under command of Major General Charles Vere Ferrers Townsend KCB, DSO found itself surrounded by Germany's allies, the Turks, in the dusty mud fort of Kut near Basra. After a lengthy siege, Townsend surrendered unconditionally and spent the rest of the war as a prisoner of the enemy. (It was a comfortable incarceration, extending even to the use of a personal yacht.) His 12,000 soldiers, on the other hand, were systematically raped, flogged, starved and murdered by their captors. Less than half of them survived to the end of the war.

Kipling's agonizing cry of anger was directed, not at the enemy, but at his country's civil and military leaders.

Mesopotamia
1917

They shall not return to us, the resolute, the young,
    The eager and whole-hearted whom we gave:
But the men who left them thriftily to die in their own dung,
    Shall they come with years and honour to the grave?

They shall not return to us; the strong men coldly slain
    In sight of help denied from day to day:
But the men who edged their agonies and chid them in their pain,
    Are they too strong and wise to put away?

Our dead shall not return to us while Day and Night divide –
    Never while the bars of sunset hold.

But the idle-minded overlings who quibbled while they died,
      Shall they thrust for high employments as of old?

Shall we only threaten and be angry for an hour:
      When the storm is ended shall we find
How softly but how swiftly they have sidled back to power
      By the favour and contrivance of their kind?

Even while they soothe us, while they promise large amends,
      Even while they make a show of fear,
Do they call upon their debtors, and take counsel with their friends,
      To conform and re-establish each career?

Their lives cannot repay us – their death could not undo –
      The shame that they have laid upon our race.
But the slothfulness that wasted and the arrogance that slew,
      Shall we leave it unabated in its place?

Miss Tompkins called the next poem an 'outcry of pain'. It asks for the return of 'the children' lost in the Great War, while at the same time acknowledging the hopelessness of the request.

The Children

The Honours of War

These were our children who died for our lands: they were dear in our sight.
> We have only the memory left of their home-treasured sayings and laughter.
> The price of our loss shall be paid to our hands, not another's hereafter.

Neither the Alien nor Priest shall decide on it. That is our right.
> *But who shall return us the children ?*

At the hour the Barbarian chose to disclose his pretences,
> And raged against Man, they engaged, on the breasts that they bared for us,
> The first felon-stroke of the sword he had longtime prepared for us -

Their bodies were all our defence while we wrought our defences.

They bought us anew with their blood, forbearing to blame us,
Those hours which we had not made good when the Judgment o'ercame us.
They believed us and perished for it. Our statecraft, our learning
Delivered them bound to the Pit and alive to the burning
Whither they mirthfully hastened as jostling for honour -
Not since her birth has our Earth seen such worth loosed upon her!

Nor was their agony brief, or once only imposed on them.
> The wounded, the war-spent, the sick received no exemption:
> Being cured they returned and endured and achieved our redemption,

Hopeless themselves of relief, till Death, marvelling, closed on them.

That flesh we had nursed from the first in all cleanness was given
To corruption unveiled and assailed by the malice of Heaven -
By the heart-shaking jests of Decay where it lolled on the wires -
To be blanched or gay-painted by fumes - to be cindered by fires -
To be senselessly tossed and retossed in stale mutilation
From crater to crater. For this we shall take expiation.
  But who shall return us our children ?

[1917]

The next poem compares a soldier in Picardy awaiting a gas attack with Christ in the garden of Gethsemane awaiting crucifixion. When his courage failed him, Jesus left his sleeping friends and prayed: 'O my Father, if it be possible, let this cup pass from me', adding, 'nevertheless not as I will, but as thou wilt.' (Matthew 26. 39, K.J.V.)

Picardy was the site of the terrible battle of the Somme in which the United Kingdom alone suffered over a third of a million casualties. Poison gas, though relatively ineffective as a weapon of war, was greatly feared by the troops for its excruciating effects on the human body.

Lord Birkenhead described the poem, as 'one of [Kipling's] 'greatest and most searing'.

Gethsemane

(1914-1918)

The Garden called Gethsemane
     In Picardy it was,
And there the people came to see
     The English soldiers pass.
We used to pass - we used to pass
     Or halt, as it might be,
And ship our masks in case of gas
     Beyond Gethsemane.

The Garden called Gethsemane,
     It held a pretty lass,
But all the time she talked to me
     I prayed my cup might pass.
The officer sat on the chair,
     The men lay on the grass,
And all the time we halted there
     I prayed my cup might pass.

It didn't pass - it didn't pass -
  It didn't pass from me.
I drank it when we met the gas
Beyond Gethsemane!

[1919]

The overriding style of the following collection of pithy epitaphs is that of the anthology known since antiquity as The Greek Collection. *Like the poems in that collection, Kipling's 'epitaphs' carry great force despite their economy of language.*

Epitaphs of the War

(1914-1918)

[A selection]

EQUALITY OF SACRIFICE

> A. "I was a Have." B. "I was a 'have-not.'"
> (Together.) "What hast thou given which I gave not?"

A SERVANT

> We were together since the War began.
> He was my servant - and the better man.

A SON

> My son was killed while laughing at some jest. I would I knew
> What it was, and it might serve me in a time when jests are few.

AN ONLY SON

> I have slain none except my Mother.
> She (Blessing her slayer) died of grief for me.

EX-CLERK

> Pity not! The Army gave
> Freedom to a timid slave:
> In which Freedom did he find
> Strength of body, will, and mind:

By which strength he came to prove
Mirth, Companionship, and Love:
For which Love to Death he went:
In which Death he lies content.

HINDU SEPOY IN FRANCE

This man in his own country prayed we know not to what Powers.
We pray Them to reward him for his bravery in ours.

THE COWARD

I could not look on Death, which being known,
Men led me to him, blindfold and alone.

SHOCK

My name, my speech, my self I had forgot.
My wife and children came - I knew them not.
I died. My Mother followed. At her call
And on her bosom I remembered all.

THE BEGINNER

On the first hour of my first day
In the front trench I fell.
(Children in boxes at a play
Stand up to watch it well.)

R.A.F. (AGED EIGHTEEN)

Laughing through clouds, his milk-teeth still unshed,
Cities and men he smote from overhead.
His deaths delivered, he returned to play
Childlike, with childish things now put away.

THE REFINED MAN

I was of delicate mind. I stepped aside for my needs,
Disdaining the common office. I was seen from afar and killed.
How is this matter for mirth? Let each man be judged by his deeds.
I have paid my price to live with myself on the terms that I willed.

BOMBED IN LONDON

On land and sea I strove with anxious care
To escape conscription. It was in the air!

THE SLEEPY SENTINEL

Faithless the watch that I kept: now I have none to keep.
I was slain because I slept: now I am slain I sleep.
Let no man reproach me again; whatever watch is unkept -
I sleep because I am slain. They slew me because I slept.

BATTERIES OUT OF AMMUNITION

If any mourn us in the workshop, say
We died because the shift kept holiday.

COMMON FORM

If any question why we died,
Tell them, because our fathers lied.

A DEAD STATESMAN

I could not dig: I dared not rob:
Therefore I lied to please the mob.
Now all my lies are proved untrue
And I must face the men I slew.
What tale shall serve me here among
Mine angry and defrauded young?

UNKNOWN FEMALE CORPSE

Headless, lacking foot and hand,
Horrible I come to land.
I beseech all women's sons
Know I was a mother once.

A DRIFTER OFF TARENTUM

He from the wind-bitten north with ship and companions descended.
Searching for eggs of death spawned by invisible hulls.
Many he found and drew forth. Of a sudden the fishery ended
In flame and a clamorous breath not new to the eye-pecking gulls.

CONVOY ESCORT

I was a shepherd to fools
Causelessly bold or afraid.
They would not abide by my rules.
Yet they escaped. For I stayed.

[1919]

V.A.D. (Mediterranean)

Ah, would swift ships had never been,[133] for then we ne'er had found,
These harsh Aegean rocks between, this little virgin drowned,
Whom neither spouse nor child shall mourn, but men she nursed through pain
And – certain keels for whose return the heathen look in vain.

---

133 This echoes Callimachus, 'Ah, would swift ships had never been about the seas to rove.'

The next poem is a rare example of Kipling's use of free verse.

On a poacher shot in no-man's land

Tom Airos the free hunter owed his country no more
than imprisonment in several gaols. In return for this,
he gave her all his skill in catching rabbits and, at the
last, his soul that abhorred imprisonment.

[1918]

Kipling described The Hyaenas *as 'a parable of newspaper attacks on dead men who cannot defend themselves'. The poem imputes no blame to the 'soulless' animals, only to the dead's own kind.*

The Hyaenas

After the burial-parties leave
  And the baffled kites have fled;
The wise hyænas come out at eve
  To take account of our dead.

How he died and why he died
  Troubles them not a whit.
They snout the bushes and stones aside
  And dig till they come to it.

They are only resolute they shall eat
  That they and their mates may thrive,
And they know that the dead are safer meat
  Than the weakest thing alive.

(For a goat may butt, and a worm may sting,
  And a child will sometimes stand;
But a poor dead soldier of the King
  Can never lift a hand.)

They whoop and halloo and scatter the dirt
  Until their tushes white
Take good hold in the army shirt,
  And tug the corpse to light,

And the pitiful face is shewn again
  For an instant ere they close;
But it is not discovered to living men -
  Only to God and to those

Who, being soulless, are free from shame,
    Whatever meat they may find.
Nor do they defile the dead man's name -
    That is reserved for his kind.

[1919]

RETURNING FROM THE WARS

At the end of his six year engagement, the Victorian soldier had only one place to go: for many it proved to be a bitter disappointment.

The narrator of Chant Pagan *rails against 'little England' and the English class system, which failed to recognize what ordinary working men were capable of.*

As to the title, Keating explains that 'paganus' was a villager or rustic liable to be enrolled in the Roman army, of inferior status to the professional soldier (or 'miles').'

Chant Pagan

(English irregular discharged)

Me that 'ave been what I've been -
Me that 'ave gone where I've gone -
Me that 'ave seen what I've seen -
     'Ow can I ever take on
With awful old England again,
An' 'ouses both sides of the street,
And 'edges two sides of the lane,
And the parson an' gentry between,
An' touchin' my 'at when we meet -
     Me that 'ave been what I've been?

Me that 'ave watched 'arf a world
'Eave up all shiny with dew,
Kopje on kop to the sun,
An' as soon as the mist let 'em through
Our 'elios winkin' like fun -
Three sides of a ninety-mile square,
Over valleys as big as a shire -
"Are ye there? Are ye there? Are ye there?"
An' then the blind drum of our fire ...
An' I'm rollin' 'is lawns for the Squire,
         Me!

Me that 'ave rode through the dark
Forty mile, often, on end,

Along the Ma'ollisberg Range,
With only the stars for my mark
An' only the night for my friend,
An' things runnin' off as you pass,
An' things jumpin' up in the grass,
An' the silence, the shine an' the size
Of the 'igh, unexpressible skies -
I am takin' some letters almost
As much as a mile to the post,
An' "mind you come back with the change!"
                              Me!

Me that saw Barberton took
When we dropped through the clouds on their 'ead,
An' they 'ove the guns over and fled -
Me that was through Di'mond 'Ill,
An' Pieters an' Springs an' Belfast -
From Dundee to Vereeniging all -
Me that stuck out to the last
(An' five bloomin' bars on my chest) -
I am doin' my Sunday-school best,
By the 'elp of the Squire an' 'is wife
(Not to mention the 'ousemaid an' cook),
To come in an' 'ands up an' be still,
An' honestly work for my bread,
My livin' in that state of life
To which it shall please Gawd to call
                              Me!

Me that 'ave followed my trade
In the place where the Lightnin's are made;
'Twixt the Rains and the Sun and the Moon -
Me that lay down an' got up
Three years with the sky for my roof -
That 'ave ridden my 'unger an' thirst
Six thousand raw mile on the hoof,
With the Vaal and the Orange for cup,

An' the Brandwater Basin for dish -
Oh! it's 'ard to be'ave as they wish
(Too 'ard, an' a little too soon),
I'll 'ave to think over it first -

                Me!

I will arise an' get 'ence -
I will trek South and make sure
If it's only my fancy or not
That the sunshine of England is pale,
And the breezes of England are stale,
An' there's something' gone small with the lot.
For *I* know of a sun an' a wind,
An' some plains and a mountain be'ind,
An' some graves by a barb-wire fence,
An' a Dutchman I've fought 'oo might give
Me a job were I ever inclined
To look in an' offsaddle an' live
Where there's neither a road nor a tree -
But only my Maker an' me,
And I think it will kill me or cure,
So I think I will go there an' see.

                Me!

[1903]

The sentiment of The Return *is similar to that of* Chant Pagan. *War has matured the soldier who has returned with an ambiguous attitude to his homeland. But what about the refrain, 'if England was what England seems'? Angus Wilson commented, 'It made nonsense of [Kipling's] political ideas and activities, although his political dreams were far from ignoble and his political nightmares often more prophetic, more persistently far-seeing than those of his more level-headed contemporaries.' But surely the emphasis placed on the last words ('But she ain't!') indicates the narrator's repudiation, however desperate, of so pessimistic a view.*

Kipling returned to the theme again in his poem, Shillin' a Day *(not included).*

The Return

(All Arms)

Peace is declared, and I return
        To 'Ackneystadt, but not the same;
Things 'ave transpired which made me learn
        The size and meanin' of the game.
I did no more than others did,
        I don't know where the change began;
I started as a average kid,
        I finished as a thinkin' man.

        If England was what England seems
                An' not the England of our dreams,
        But only putty, brass, an' paint,
                'Ow quick we'd drop 'er! But she ain't!

Before my gappin' mouth could speak
        I 'eard it in my comrade's tone;
I saw it on my neighbour's cheek
        Before I felt it flush my own.
An' last it come to me - not pride,
        Nor yet conceit, but on the 'ole

153

(If such a term may be applied),
        The makin's of a bloomin' soul.

Rivers at night that cluck an' jeer,
        Plains which the moonshine turns to sea,
Mountains that never let you near,
        An' stars to all eternity;
An' the quick-breathin' dark that fills
        The 'ollows of the wilderness,
When the wind worries through the 'ills -
        These may 'ave taught me more or less.

Towns without people, ten times took,
        An' ten times left an' burned at last;
An' starvin' dogs that come to look
        For owners when a column passed;
An' quiet, 'omesick talks between
        Men, met by night, you never knew
Until - 'is face - by shellfire seen -
        Once - an' struck off. *They* taught me, too.

The day's lay-out - the mornin' sun
        Beneath your 'at-brim as you sight;
The dinner-'ush from noon till one,
        An' the full roar that lasts till night;
An' the pore dead that look so old
        An' was so young an hour ago,
An' legs tied down before they're cold -
        These are the things which make you know.

Also Time runnin' into years -
        A thousand Places left be'ind -
An' Men from both two 'emispheres
        Discussin' things of every kind;
So much more near than I 'ad known,
        So much more great than I 'ad guessed -

An' me, like all the rest, alone -
       But reachin' out to all the rest!

So 'ath it come to me - not pride,
       Nor yet conceit, but on the 'ole
(If such a term may be applied),
       The makin's of a bloomin' soul.
But now, discharged, I fall away
       To do with little things again ....
Gawd, 'oo knows all I cannot say,
       Look after me in Thamesfontein!

If England was what England seems
       An' not the England of our dreams,
But only putty, brass, an' paint,
       'Ow quick we'd chuck 'er! But she ain't!

[1903]

Although set during the Second Boer War, Lichtenberg *is not about conflict, but memory. Kipling had an exceptional ability to evoke a place, a smell, a moment. Here an Australian veteran of the war recollects the small things that stuck in his memory from a time when he was stationed far from the fighting.*

It is only one of the many poems which refute the notion that Kipling was incapable of lyric expression.

Lichtenberg

(New South Wales Contingent)

Smells are surer than sounds or sights
 To make your heart-strings crack -
They start those awful voices o' nights
 That whisper, "Old man, come back!"
That must be why the big things pass
 And the little things remain,
Like the smell of the wattle by Lichtenberg,
 Riding in, in the rain.

There was some silly fire on the flank
 And the small wet drizzling down -
There were the sold-out shops and the bank
 And the wet, wide-open town;
And we were doing escort-duty
 To somebody's baggage-train,
And I smelt wattle by Lichtenberg -
 Riding in, in the rain.

It was all Australia to me -
 All I had found or missed:
Every face I was crazy to see,
 And every woman I'd kissed:
All that I shouldn't ha' done, God knows!
 (As He knows I'll do it again),

That smell of the wattle round Lichtenberg,
Riding in, in the rain!

And I saw Sydney the same as ever,
The picnics and brass-bands;
And my little homestead on Hunter River
And my new vines joining hands.
It all came over me in one act
Quick as a shot through the brain -
With the smell of the wattle round Lichtenberg,
Riding in, in the rain.

I have forgotten a hundred fights,
But one I shall not forget -
With the raindrops bunging up my sights
And my eyes bunged up with wet;
And through the crack and the stink of the cordite
(Ah Christ! My country again!)
The smell of the wattle by Lichtenberg,
Riding in, in the rain!

[1903]

HEALING

The concept of healing, spiritual and physical, is one with which the mature Kipling became increasingly concerned.

This section begins with the healing which takes place after a war, when former enemies have to face up to little Peterkin's question, 'But what good came of it at last?'[134]

134 Southey. *The Battle of Blenheim.*

In war even the healers are at risk. The novelist, Mary Hamer tells us that ninety nine nurses served with the British army in South Africa and that Kipling visited many of the hospitals in which they worked, taking dictation from those too ill to write home for themselves.[135] Lord Birkenhead considered the following threnody to be 'one of the finest rhetorical poems Kipling ever wrote.'

"Dirge of Dead Sisters"

1902

(For the Nurses who died in the South African War)

Who recalls the twilight and the rangèd tents in order
    (Violet peaks uplifted through the crystal evening air?)
And the clink of iron teacups and the piteous, noble laughter,
    And the faces of the Sisters with the dust upon their hair?

(Now and not hereafter, while the breath is in our nostrils,
    Now and not hereafter, ere the meaner years go by -
Let us now remember many honourable women,
    Such as bade us turn again when we were like to die.)

Who recalls the morning and the thunder through the foothills
    (Tufts of fleecy shrapnel strung along the empty plains?)
And the sun-scarred Red-Cross coaches creeping guarded to the culvert,
    And the faces of the Sisters looking gravely from the trains?

(When the days were torment and the nights were clouded terror,
    When the Powers of Darkness had dominion on our soul -
When we fled consuming through the Seven Hells of Fever,
    These put out their hands to us and healed and made us whole.)

Who recalls the midnight by the bridge's wrecked abutment
    (Autumn rain that rattled like a Maxim on the tin?)

---

135 Kipling Society Readers' Guide.

And the lightning-dazzled levels and the streaming, straining wagons,
 And the faces of the Sisters as they bore the wounded in?

(Till the pain was merciful and stunned us into silence -
 When each nerve cried out on God that made the misused clay;
When the Body triumphed and the last poor shame departed -
 These abode our agonies and wiped the sweat away.)

Who recalls the noontide and the funerals through the market
 (Blanket-hidden bodies, flagless, followed by the flies?)
And the footsore firing-party, and the dust and stench and staleness,
 And the faces of the Sisters and the glory in their eyes?

(Bold behind the battle, in the open camp all-hallowed,
 Patient, wise, and mirthful in the ringed and reeking town,
These endured unresting till they rested from their labours -
 Little wasted bodies, ah, so light to lower down!)

Yet their graves are scattered and their names are clean forgotten,
 Earth shall not remember, but the Waiting Angel knows
Them that died at Uitvlugt when the plague was on the city -
 Her that fell at Simon's Town in service on our foes.

Wherefore we they ransomed, while the breath is in our nostrils;
 Now and not hereafter - ere the meaner years go by -
Praise with love and worship many honourable women,
 Those that gave their lives for us when we were like to die!

Britain did not emerge from the second Boer war covered in glory. As Kipling wrote in his poem, The Lesson *(not included), 'Let us admit it fairly as a business people should,/We have had no end of a lesson; it will do us no end of good.' But, as the poet knew, the first priority was reconciliation between former enemies.*

The Settler

1903

(South African War ended, May 1902)

Here, where my fresh-turned furrows run,
    And the deep soil glistens red,
I will repair the wrong that was done
    To the living and the dead.
Here, where the senseless bullet fell,
    And the barren shrapnel burst,
I will plant a tree, I will dig a well,
    Against the heat and the thirst.

Here, in a large and sunlit land
    Where no wrong bites to the bone,
I will lay my hand in my neighbour's hand,
    And together we will atone
For the set folly and the red breach
    And the black waste of it all;
Giving and taking counsel each
    Over the cattle-kraal.

Here we will join against our foes -
    The hailstroke and the storm,
And the red and rustling cloud that blows
    The locust's mile-deep storm.
Frost and murrain and flood let loose
    Shall launch us side by side
In the holy wars that have no truce
    'Twixt seed and harvest-tide.

Earth where we rode to slay or be slain,
    Our love shall redeem unto life.
We will gather and lead to her lips again
    The waters of ancient strife.
From the far and the fiercely guarded streams
    And the pools where we lay in wait
Till the corn cover our evil dreams
    And the young corn our hate.

And when we bring old fights to mind,
    We will not remember the sin -
If there be blood on his head of my kind,
    Or blood on my head of his kin -
For the ungrazed upland, the untilled lea
    Cry, and the fields forlorn:
"The dead must bury their dead, but ye -
    Ye serve a host unborn."

Bless then, Our God, the new-yoked plough
And the good beasts that draw,
    And the bread we eat in the sweat of our brow
        According to Thy Law.
After us cometh a multitude -
    Prosper the work of our hands,
That we may feed with our land's food
    The folk of all our lands!

Here, in the waves and the troughs of the plains,
    Where the healing stillness lies,
And the vast benignant sky restrains
    And the long days make wise -
Bless to our use the rain and the sun
    And the blind seed in its bed,
That we may repair the wrong that was done
    To the living and the dead!

Though written to accompany a short story about an American couple who settle in England[136], the next poem seems equally appropriate to the poet's own rediscovery of his native country upon returning from Vermont in which the very land is seen as capable of conducting a process akin to healing.

The Recall

I am the land of their fathers,
In me the virtue stays.
I will bring back my children,
After certain days.

Under their feet in the grasses
My clinging magic runs.
They shall return as strangers.
They shall remain as sons.

Over their heads in the branches
Of their new-bought, ancient trees,
I weave an incantation
And draw them to my knees.

Scent of smoke in the evening,
Smell of rain in the night -
The hours, the days and the seasons,
Order their souls aright,

Till I make plain the meaning
Of all my thousand years
Till I fill their hearts with knowledge,
While I fill their eyes with tears.

[1909]

---

136   An Habitation Enforced.

For Kipling, the discovery of Bateman's and Sussex began a process which he describes in A Charm, *using folk medicine as a metaphor for healing.*

A Charm

(Introduction to *Rewards and Fairies*)

Take of English earth as much
As either hand may rightly clutch.
In the taking of it breathe
Prayer for all who lie beneath.
Not the great nor well-bespoke,
But the mere uncounted folk
Of whose life and death is none
Report or lamentation.
      Lay that earth upon thy heart,
      And thy sickness shall depart!

It shall sweeten and make whole
Fevered breath and festered soul.
It shall mightily restrain
Over-busied hand and brain,
It shall ease thy mortal strife
'Gainst the immortal woe of life,
Till thyself, restored, shall prove
By what grace the Heavens do move.
Take of English flowers these
Spring's full-faced primroses,
Summer's wild wide-hearted rose,
Autumn's wall-flower of the close,
And, thy darkness to illume,
Winter's bee-thronged ivy-bloom.
Seek and serve them where they bide
From Candlemas to Christmas-tide,
      For these simples, used aright,
      Can restore a failing sight.

These shall cleanse and purify
Webbed and inward-turning eye;
These shall show thee treasure hid
Thy familiar fields amid;
At thy threshold, on thy hearth,
Or about thy daily path;
And reveal (which is thy need)
Every man a King indeed!

[1910]

Valley Forge in Pennsylvania was the winter camp for the American rebel army throughout the bitter winter of 1777-1778. Though never attacked, the men lived in conditions of great hunger, cold and privation. This beautiful poem of reconciliation is Kipling's memorial to the dead of both sides.

Like Shakespeare, Kipling often turned to flowers to convey his strongest emotions.

The American rebellion

(1776)

AFTER

The snow lies thick on Valley Forge,
        The ice on the Delaware,
But the poor dead soldiers of King George
        They neither know nor care.

Nor though the earliest primrose break
        On the sunny side of the lane,
And scuffling rookeries awake
        Their England's spring again.

They will not stir when the drifts are gone,
        Or the ice melts out of the bay:
And the men that served with Washington
        Lie as still as they.

They will not stir though the mayflower blows
        In the moist dark woods of pine,
And every rock-strewn pasture shows
        Mullein and Columbine.

Each for his land, in a fair fight,
        Encountered, strove, and died,

And the kindly earth that knows no spite
        Covers them side by side.

She is too busy to think of war;
        She has all the world to make gay;
And, behold, the yearly flowers are
        Where they were in our fathers' day!

Golden-rod by the pasture wall
        When the columbine is dead,
And sumach leaves that turn, in fall,
        Bright as the blood they shed.

[1911]

When he wrote the next poem Kipling had begun to be seriously concerned about his health. He admired the medical profession and had many of its members among his friends. The Kipling Society lists twenty of his stories as relating to "Doctors or Medicine", and twenty-five to "Healing".

Doctors

1923

Man dies too soon, beside his works half-planned.
      His days are counted and reprieve is vain:
Who shall entreat with Death to stay his hand;
      Or cloke the shameful nakedness of pain?

Send here the bold, the seekers of the way -
      The passionless, the unshakeable of soul,
Who serve the inmost mysteries of man's clay,
      And ask no more than leave to make them whole.

London Stone rejects the Biblical assertion that death has no dominion over us. At the time of remembrance particularly, we must 'tell no lie', but accept that grieving is the real sting of death; its only consolation, the suffering of our fellows.

The London Stone has been a feature of the City for centuries. It is now exposed in the wall of a building in Cannon Street. Its origins are lost in legend. The date of the poem is Remembrance Day.

London Stone

(November 11, 1923)

When you come to London Town,
    (Grieving-grieving!)
Bring your flowers and lay them down
    At the place of grieving.

When you come to London Town,
    (Grieving-grieving!)
Bow your head and mourn your own,
    With the others grieving.

For those minutes, let it wake,
    (Grieving-grieving!)
All the empty-heart and ache
    That is not cured by grieving.

For those minutes, tell no lie:
    (Grieving-grieving!)
"Grave, this is thy victory;
    And the sting of death is grieving."

Where's our help, from Earth or Heaven,
    (Grieving-grieving!)
To comfort us for what we've given,
    And only gained this grieving?

Heaven's too far and Earth too near,
      (Grieving-grieving!)
But our neighbour's standing here,
      Grieving as we're grieving.

What's his burden every day?
      (Grieving-grieving!)
Nothing man can count or weigh,
      But loss and love's own grieving.

What is the tie betwixt us two
      (Grieving-grieving!)
That must last our whole lives through?
      "As I suffer, so do you."
      That may ease the grieving.

The Burden *was designed to be read along with* The Gardener, *one of Kipling's finest stories. In this, its final form, the first four stanzas are spoken by the story's central character, Helen; the fifth by Mary Magdalene.*

Although not strictly a poem of healing, The Burden *is, in the words of Miss J.M.S. Tompkins, a poem 'of infinite compassion'.*

The Burden

The Gardener

One grief on me is laid
     Each day of every year,
Wherein no soul can aid,
     Whereof no soul can hear:
Whereto no end is seen
     Except to grieve again -
Ah, Mary Magdalene,
     Where is there greater pain?

To dream on dear disgrace
     Each hour of every day -
To bring no honest face
     To aught I do or say:
To lie from morn till e'en -
     To know my lies are vain -
Ah, Mary Magdalene,
     Where can be greater pain?

To watch my steadfast fear
     Attend mine every way
Each day of every year -
     Each hour of every day:
To burn, and chill between -
     To quake and rage again -
Ah, Mary Magdalene,
     Where shall be greater pain?

One grave to me was given -
        To guard till Judgment Day -
But God looked down from Heaven
        And rolled the Stone away!
One day of all my years -
        One hour of that one day -
His Angel saw my tears
        And rolled the Stone away!

[1926]

EXPLORATION AND DISCOVERY

For all his life Kipling experienced an urge to travel, to explore, to push the boundaries of geography, science and technology; and he wrote at length about what he found. When, in 1922, senior members of the Canadian engineering profession decided that they needed a ceremony for graduating members, they turned naturally to Kipling. His response was *'The Ritual of the Calling of an Engineer'* (not included). The Kipling ritual, as it is sometimes called, is still in use today.

Kipling the man had a yen for inclusivity, whether in a club, a secret society like the Masons, or a closed circle such as the fellowship of journalists and soldiers. Part of the pleasure for him was access to their insiders' language, the terms of their trade. Some, like the poet, Richard Le Gallienne, have condemned Kipling's obsession with this, his 'merciless technicalities'. It is a fair comment, but we must remember that Kipling was not writing text books, but trying to give the feel of what it is like to be on the inside of a trade or closed group.

TECHNOLOGY AND THE SEA

In Kipling's day some of the most exciting manifestations of technology were to be found at sea. His poem, *McAndrew's Hymn* (a monologue from the Chief Engineer of a cargo-liner, not included) begins,

Lord, Thou hast made this world below the shadow of a dream,
An', taught by time, I tak' it so - exceptin' always Steam.
From coupler-flange to spindle-guide I see Thy Hand, O God -
Predestination in the stride o' yon connectin'-rod.
John Calvin might ha' forged the same - enormous, certain, slow -
Ay, wrought it in the furnace-flame - my "Institutio."[137]

But the poet never lost sight of the limitations of technology. In *The Secret of the Machines* (not included) he wrote:

Though our smoke may hide the Heavens from your eyes,
It will vanish and the stars will shine again,
Because, for all our power and weight and size,
We are nothing more than children of your brain!

137   Calvin's Institutes of the Christian Religion was his great work on Protestant theology.

The Ballad of the Bolivar *is a tale of seven cheery sailors whose heroism saved an ill founded ship from the sea. The phrase, 'meant to founder' implies that the Bolivar was a 'coffin-ship', over-insured by its owners and intended for the deeps.*

Ballad of the Bolivar

1890

Seven men from all the world, back to Docks again,
Rolling down the Ratcliffe Road drunk and raising Cain:
Give the girls another drink 'fore we sign away -
We that took the "Bolivar" out across the Bay!

We put out from Sunderland loaded down with rails;
      We put back to Sunderland 'cause our cargo shifted;
We put out from Sunderland - met the winter gales -
      Seven days and seven nights to the Start we drifted.

      Racketing her rivets loose, smoke-stack white as snow,
      All the coals adrift adeck, half the rails below,
      Leaking like a lobster-pot, steering like a dray -
      Out we took the Bolivar, out across the Bay!

One by one the Lights came up, winked and let us by;
      Mile by mile we waddled on, coal and fo'c'sle short;
Met a blow that laid us down, heard a bulkhead fly;
      Left the Wolf behind us with a two-foot list to port.

      Trailing like a wounded duck, working out her soul;
      Clanging like a smithy-shop after every roll;
      Just a funnel and a mast lurching through the spray -
      So we threshed the Bolivar out across the Bay!

'Felt her hog and felt her sag, betted when she'd break;
      'Wondered every time she raced if she'd stand the shock;

'Heard the seas like drunken men pounding at her strake;
      'Hoped the Lord 'ud keep his thumb on the plummer-block.

      Banged against the iron decks, bilges choked with coal;
      Flayed and frozen foot and hand, sick of heart and soul;
      'Last we prayed she'd buck herself into judgment Day -
      Hi! we cursed the Bolivar knocking round the Bay!

Oh, her nose flung up to sky, groaning to be still -
      Up and down and back we went, never time for breath;
Then the money paid at Lloyd's caught her by the keel,
      And the stars ran round and round dancin' at our death!

      Aching for an hour's sleep, dozing off between;
      'Heard the rotten rivets draw when she took it green;
      'Watched the compass chase its tail like a cat at play -
      That was on the Bolivar, south across the Bay!

Once we saw between the squalls, lyin' head to swell -
      Mad with work and weariness, wishin' they was we -
Some damned Liner's lights go by like a long hotel;
      Cheered her from the Bolivar swampin' in the sea.

      Then a grayback cleared us out, then the skipper laughed;
      "Boys, the wheel has gone to Hell - rig the winches aft!
      Yoke the kicking rudder-head - get her under way!"
      So we steered her, pulley-haul, out across the Bay!

Just a pack o' rotten plates puttied up with tar,
In we came, an' time enough, 'cross Bilbao Bar.
Overloaded, undermanned, meant to founder, we
Euchred God Almighty's storm, bluffed the Eternal Sea!

      Seven men from all the world, back to Town again,
      Rollin' down the Ratcliffe Road drunk and raising Cain:
      Seven men from out of Hell. Ain't the owners gay,
      'Cause we took the Bolivar safe across the Bay?

The Deep-sea Cables *was written in optimistic mood to commemorate the projected trans-oceanic cable.*

For a poem which deals with such mundane inventions as the electric telegraph and the Morse code its atmosphere is eerily romantic.

The Deep-sea Cables

The wrecks dissolve above us; their dust drops down from afar -
Down to the dark, to the utter dark, where the blind white sea-snakes are.
There is no sound, no echo of sound, in the deserts of the deep,
Or the great grey level plains of ooze where the shell-burred cables creep.

Here in the womb of the world - here on the tie-ribs of earth -
      Words, and the words of men, flicker and flutter and beat -
Warning, sorrow and gain, salutation and mirth -
      For a Power troubles the Still that has neither voice nor feet.

They have wakened the timeless Things; they have killed their father Time;
      Joining hands in the gloom, a league from the last of the sun.
Hush! Men talk to-day o'er the waste of the ultimate slime,
      And a new Word runs between: whispering, 'Let us be one!'

[1893]

An island nation must be a seafaring one or perish. But there is always a price to pay.

The effect of the next poem is reinforced by the increasing repetition of the term, 'the price of admiralty'.

The Song of the Dead

II

We have fed our sea for a thousand years
        And she calls us, still unfed,
Though there's never a wave of all her waves
        But marks our English dead:
We have strawed our best to the weed's unrest,
        To the shark and the sheering gull.
If blood be the price of admiralty,
        Lord God, we ha' paid in full!

There's never a flood goes shoreward now
        But lifts a keel we manned;
There's never an ebb goes seaward now
        But drops our dead on the sand -
But slinks our dead on the sands forlore,
        From the Ducies to the Swin.
If blood be the price of admiralty,
If blood be the price of admiralty,
        Lord God, we ha' paid it in!

We must feed our sea for a thousand years,
        For that is our doom and pride,
As it was when they sailed with the *Golden Hind*,
        Or the wreck that struck last tide -
Or the wreck that lies on the spouting reef
        Where the ghastly blue-lights flare.

If blood be the price of admiralty,
If blood be the price of admiralty,
If blood be the price of admiralty,
      Lord God, we ha' bought it fair!

[1893]

Since the earliest times fortunes have been made and lost at sea.

In The Mary Gloster *a dying shipping magnate addresses the son who has been such a disappointment to him. He boasts of his successes and confesses his sharp practices. He has not always been faithful to his wife, but it was she with whom he wishes to be united in death.*

The Mary Gloster *is a monologue after the style of Browning's* The Bishop Orders His Tomb at Saint Praxed's Church. *It is a companion piece to the better known* McAndrew's Hymn, *and in the present editor's view the better of the two. Henry James described the 'coarseness' of this poem as 'absolutely one of the most triumphant 'values' of that triumphant thing.'138*

The *Mary Gloster*

1894

I've paid for your sickest fancies; I've humoured your crackedest whim -
Dick, it's your daddy, dying; you've got to listen to him!
Good for a fortnight, am I? The doctor told you? He lied.
I shall go under by morning, and - Put that nurse outside.
'Never seen death yet, Dickie? Well, now is your time to learn,
And you'll wish you held my record before it comes to your turn.
Not counting the Line and the Foundry, the Yards and the village, too,
I've made myself and a million; but I'm damned if I made you.
Master at two-and-twenty, and married at twenty-three -
Ten thousand men on the pay-roll, and forty freighters at sea!
Fifty years between 'em, and every year of it fight,
And now I'm Sir Anthony Gloster, dying, a baronite:
For I lunched with his Royal 'Ighness - what was it the papers had?
"Not least of our merchant-princes." Dickie, that's me, your dad!
I didn't begin with askings. I took my job and I stuck;
And I took the chances they wouldn't, an' now they're calling it luck.
Lord, what boats I've handled - rotten and leaky and old -
Ran 'em, or - opened the bilge-cock, precisely as I was told.

---

138 Letter to Jonathan Sturges, 5 November 1986.

182

Grub that 'ud bind you crazy, and crews that 'ud turn you grey,
And a big fat lump of insurance to cover the risk on the way.
The others they dursn't do it; they said they valued their life
(They've served me since as skippers). I went, and I took my wife.
Over the world I drove 'em, married at twenty-three,
And your mother saving the money and making a man of me.
I was content to be master, but she said there was better behind;
She took the chances I wouldn't, and I followed your mother blind.
She egged me to borrow the money, an' she helped me to clear the loan,
When we bought half shares in a cheap 'un and hoisted a flag of our own.
Patching and coaling on credit, and living the Lord knew how,
We started the Red Ox freighters -we've eight-and-thirty now.
And those were the days of clippers, and the freights were clipper-freights,
And we knew we were making our fortune, but she died in Macassar
Straits -
By the Little Paternosters, as you come to the Union Bank -
And we dropped her in fourteen fathom; I pricked it off where she sank.
Owners we were, full owners, and the boat was christened for her,
And she died in the *Mary Gloster*. My heart, how young we were!
So I went on a spree round Java and well-nigh ran her ashore,
But your mother came and warned me and I wouldn't liquor no more:
Strict I stuck to my business, afraid to stop or I'd think,
Saving the money (she warned me), and letting the other men drink.
And I met M'Cullough in London (I'd saved five 'undred then),
And 'tween us we started the Foundry - three forges and twenty men:
Cheap repairs for the cheap 'uns. It paid, and the business grew,
For I bought me a steam-lathe patent, and that was a gold mine too.
"Cheaper to build 'em than buy 'em," I said, but M'Cullough he shied,
And we wasted a year in talking before we moved to the Clyde.
And the Lines were all beginning, and we all of us started fair,
Building our engines like houses and staying the boilers square.
But M'Cullough 'e wanted cabins with marble and maple and all,
And Brussels an' Utrecht velvet, and baths and a Social Hall,
And pipes for closets all over, and cutting the frames too light,
But M'Cullough he died in the Sixties, and - Well, I'm dying to-night....
I knew—I knew what was coming, when we bid on the *Byfleet's* keel -
They piddled and piffled with iron: I'd given my orders for steel!

Steel and the first expansions. It paid, I tell you, it paid,
When we came with our nine-knot freighters and collared the long-run trade!
And they asked me how I did it, and I gave 'em the Scripture text,
"You keep your light so shining a little in front o' the next!"
They copied all they could follow, but they couldn't copy my mind,
And I left 'em sweating and stealing a year and a half behind.
Then came the armour-contracts, but that was M'Cullough's side;
He was always best in the Foundry, but better, perhaps, he died.
I went through his private papers; the notes was plainer than print;
And I'm no fool to finish if a man'll give me a hint.
(I remember his widow was angry.) So I saw what the drawings meant,
And I started the six-inch rollers, and it paid me sixty per cent—
Sixty per cent *with* failures, and more than twice we could do,
And a quarter-million to credit, and I saved it all for you!
I thought - it doesn't matter - you seemed to favour your ma,
But you're nearer forty than thirty, and I know the kind you are.
Harrer an' Trinity College! I ought to ha' sent you to sea -
But I stood you an education, an' what have you done for me?
The things I knew was proper you wouldn't thank me to give,
And the things I knew was rotten you said was the way to live.
For you muddled with books and pictures, an' china an' etchin's an' fans,
And your rooms at college was beastly - more like a whore's than a man's -
Till you married that thin-flanked woman, as white and as stale as a bone,
An' she gave you your social nonsense; but where's that kid o' your own?
I've seen your carriages blocking the half o' the Cromwell Road,
But never the doctor's brougham to help the missus unload.
(So there isn't even a grandchild, an' the Gloster family's done.)
Not like your mother, she isn't. *She* carried her freight each run.
But they died, the pore little beggars! At sea she had 'em - they died.
Only you, an' you stood it; you haven't stood much beside.
Weak, a liar, and idle, and mean as a collier's whelp
Nosing for scraps in the galley. No help -my son was no help!
So he gets three 'undred thousand, in trust and the interest paid.
I wouldn't give it you, Dickie - you see, I made it in trade.
You're saved from soiling your fingers, and if you have no child,
It all comes back to the business. Gad, won't your wife be wild!

'Calls and calls in her carriage, her 'andkerchief up to 'er eye:
"Daddy! dear daddy's dyin'!" and doing her best to cry.
Grateful? Oh, yes, I'm grateful, but keep her away from here.
Your mother 'ud never ha' stood 'er, and, anyhow, women are queer ...
There's women will say I've married a second time.
Not quite! But give pore Aggie a hundred, and tell her your lawyers'll fight.
She was the best o' the boiling - you'll meet her before it ends;
I'm in for a row with the mother - I'll leave you settle my friends:
For a man he must go with a woman, which women don't understand -
Or the sort that say they can see it they aren't the marrying brand.
But I wanted to speak o' your mother that's Lady Gloster still -
I'm going to up and see her, without it's hurting the will.
Here! Take your hand off the bell-pull. Five thousand's waiting for you,
If you'll only listen a minute, and do as I bid you do.
They'll try to prove me crazy, and, if you bungle, they can;
And I've only you to trust to! (O God, why ain't he a man?)
There's some waste money on marbles, the same as M'Cullough tried -
Marbles and mausoleums - but I call that sinful pride.
There's some ship bodies for burial - we've carried 'em, soldered and packed;
Down in their wills they wrote it, and nobody called them cracked.
But me - I've too much money, and people might. ... All my fault:
It come o' hoping for grandsons and buying that Wokin' vault.
I'm sick o' the 'ole dam' business; I'm going back where I came.
Dick, you're the son o' my body, and you'll take charge o' the same!
I want to lie by your mother, ten thousand mile away,
And they'll want to send me to Woking; and that's where you'll earn your pay.
I've thought it out on the quiet, the same as it ought to be done -
Quiet, and decent, and proper - an' here's your orders, my son.
You know the Line? You don't, though. You write to the Board, and tell
Your father's death has upset you an' you're goin' to cruise for a spell,
An' you'd like the *Mary Gloster* - I've held her ready for this -
They'll put her in working order and you'll take her out as she is.
Yes, it was money idle when I patched her and put her aside
(Thank God, I can pay for my fancies!) - the boat where your mother died,
By the Little Paternosters, as you come to the Union Bank,

185

We dropped her - I think I told you - and I pricked it off where she sank -
['Tiny she looked on the grating - that oily, treacly sea -]
'Hundred and eighteen East, remember, and South just three.
Easy bearings to carry - three South - three to the dot;
But I gave M'Andrew a copy in case of dying - or not.
And so you'll write to M'Andrew, he's Chief of the Maori Line;
They'll give him leave, if you ask 'em and say it's business o' mine.
I built three boats for the Maoris, an' very well pleased they were,
An' I've known Mac since the Fifties, and Mac knew me - and her.
After the first stroke warned me I sent him the money to keep
Against the time you'd claim it, committin' your dad to the deep;
For you are the son o' my body, and Mac was my oldest friend,
I've never asked 'im to dinner, but he'll see it out to the end.
Stiff-necked Glasgow beggar, I've heard he's prayed for my soul,
But he couldn't lie if you paid him, and he'd starve before he stole!
He'll take the *Mary* in ballast - you'll find her a lively ship;
And you'll take Sir Anthony Gloster, that goes on 'is wedding-trip,
Lashed in our old deck-cabin with all three port-holes wide,
The kick o' the screw beneath him and the round blue seas outside!
Sir Anthony Gloster's carriage - our 'ouse-flag flyin' free -
Ten thousand men on the pay-roll and forty freighters at sea!
He made himself and a million, but this world is a fleetin' show,
And he'll go to the wife of 'is bosom the same as he ought to go -
By the heel of the Paternosters - there isn't a chance to mistake -
And Mac'll pay you the money as soon as the bubbles break!
Five thousand for six weeks' cruising, the staunchest freighter afloat,
And Mac he'll give you your bonus the minute I'm out o' the boat!
He'll take you round to Macassar, and you'll come back alone;
He knows what I want o' the *Mary* ... I'll do what I please with my own.
Your mother 'ud call it wasteful, but I've seven-and-thirty more;
I'll come in my private carriage and bid it wait at the door ...
For my son 'e was never a credit: 'e muddled with books and art,
And 'e lived on Sir Anthony's money and 'e broke Sir Anthony's heart.
There isn't even a grandchild, and the Gloster family's done -
The only one you left me, O mother, the only one!
Harrer and Trinity College - me slavin' early an' late -
An' he thinks I'm dying crazy, and you're in Macassar Strait!

Flesh o' my flesh, my dearie, for ever an' ever amen,
That first stroke come for a warning; I ought to ha' gone to you then,
But - cheap repairs for a cheap 'un - the doctors said I'd do:
Mary, why didn't *you* warn me? I've allus heeded to you,
Excep' - I know - about women; but you are a spirit now;
An', wife, they was only women, and I was a man. That's how.
An' a man 'e must go with a woman, as you *could* not understand;
But I never talked 'em secrets. I paid 'em out o' hand.
Thank Gawd, I can pay for my fancies! Now what's five thousand to me,
For a berth off the Paternosters in the haven where I would be?
I believe in the Resurrection, if I read my Bible plain,
But I wouldn't trust 'em at Wokin'; we're safer at sea again.
For the heart it shall go with the treasure - go down to the sea in ships.
I'm sick of the hired women - I'll kiss my girl on her lips!
I'll be content with my fountain, I'll drink from my own well,
And the wife of my youth shall charm me - an' the rest can go to Hell!
(Dickie, *he* will, that's certain.) I'll lie in our standin'-bed,
An' Mac'll take her in ballast - an' she trims best by the head ...
Down by the head an' sinkin', her fires are drawn and cold,
And the water's splashin' hollow on the skin of the empty hold -
Churning an' choking and chuckling, quiet and scummy and dark -
Full to her lower hatches and risin' steady. Hark!
That was the after-bulkhead ... She's flooded from stem to stern ...
Never seen death yet, Dickie? ... Well, now is your time to learn!

Harp Song of the Dane Women *is a lament by the women who in Summer are deserted by their men who cross the dangerous seas in search of adventure and treasure. It is generally regarded as one of Kipling's finest poems. Although written as an accompaniment to one of his children's stories, Christopher Hitchens was of opinion that it 'expressed something profound about men and women and warfare.'*[139]

Harp Song of the Dane Women

What is a woman that you forsake her,
  And the hearth-fire and the home-acre,
  For to go with the old grey Widow-maker?

She has no house to lay a guest in -
But one chill bed for all to rest in,
That the pale suns and the stray bergs nest in.

She has no strong white arms to fold you,
But the ten-times-fingering weed to hold you -
Bound on the rocks where the tide has rolled you.

Yet, when the signs of summer thicken,
  And the ice breaks, and the birch-buds quicken,
  Then yearly you turn from our side, and sicken -

Sicken again for the shouts and the slaughters, -
You steal away to the lapping waters,
And you look at your ship in her winter quarters.

You forget our mirth, and our talk at the tables,
  The kine in the shed and the horse in the stables -
  For to pitch her sides and go over her cables!

---

139 Hitchins. *Atlantic Monthly.* June 2002.

Then you drive out where the storm-clouds swallow:
 And the sound of your oar-blades falling hollow,
Is all we have left through the months to follow.

Ah, what is a woman that you forsake her,
And the hearth-fire and the home-acre,
For to go with the old grey Widow-maker?

[1906]

The next little gem of a poem has, like much of Kipling's verse, been put to music by various composers, including Edward Elgar. It describes in the plainest of terms a military engagement in which success is measured by the lack of casualties.

Mine Sweepers

Dawn off the Foreland - the young flood making
    Jumbled and short and steep -
Black in the hollows and bright where it's breaking -
    Awkward water to sweep.
    "Mines reported in the fairway,
    Warn all traffic and detain.
'Sent up *Unity, Claribel, Assyrian, Stormcock,* and *Golden Gain.*"

Noon off the Foreland - the first ebb making
    Lumpy and strong in the bight.
Boom after boom, and the golf-hut shaking
    And the jackdaws wild with fright!
    "Mines located in the fairway,
    Boats now working up the chain,
"Sweepers - *Unity, Claribel, Assyrian, Stormcock,* and *Golden Gain.*"

Dusk off the Foreland - the last light going
    And the traffic crowding through,
And five damned trawlers with their syreens blowing
    Heading the whole review!
    "Sweep completed in the fairway.
    No more mines remain.
'Sent back *Unity, Claribel, Assyrian, Stormcock,* and *Golden Gain.*"

[1915]

Submarines have seldom been the subject of poetry, but the images in the following poem ('the belly of death' and 'the mirth of a seaport') make it one of Kipling's most memorable short pieces of the war.

"Tin Fish"

The ships destroy us above
    And ensnare us beneath.
We arise, we lie down, and we move
    In the belly of Death.

The ships have a thousand eyes
    To mark where we come ...
But the mirth of a seaport dies
    When our blow gets home.

[1915]

There are few environments more hostile than the ocean. When it chooses to test its passengers, duty and training tell, even on the part of landlubbers.

'The Sarah Sands' was a steamer which was taking the 54th Regiment of Foot to India during the Mutiny of 1857. In the middle of the Indian Ocean, some 800 miles from land, fire broke out in the hold. Fearing that the gunpowder on board would explode, the newly recruited civilian crew abandoned ship. It was left to the soldiers to get the women and children into the lifeboats and throw the gunpowder kegs overboard, followed by the already burning coal. They even managed to save the regimental colours. Throughout this hazardous enterprise they could never have been certain when their time was up.

The Last Lap

The Burning of the Sarah Sands

How do we know, by the bank-high river,
    Where the mired and sulky oxen wait,
And it looks as though we might wait for ever,
    How do we know that the floods abate?
There is no change in the current's brawling -
    Louder and harsher the freshet scolds;
Yet we can feel she is falling, falling
    And the more she threatens the less she holds,
Down to the drift, with no word spoken,
    The wheel-chained wagons slither and slue ...
Achtung! The back of the worst is broken!
    And - lash your leaders! - we're through - we're through!

How do we know, when the port-fog holds us
    Moored and helpless, a mile from the pier,
And the week-long summer smother enfolds us -
    How do we know it is going to clear?
There is no break in the blindfold weather,

But, one and another, about the bay,
The unseen capstans clink together,
    Getting ready to up and away.
A pennon whimpers - the breeze has found us -
    A headsail jumps through the thinning haze.
The whole hull follows, till - broad around us -
    The clean-swept ocean says: "Go your ways!"

How do we know, when the long fight rages,
    On the old, stale front that we cannot shake,
And it looks as though we were locked for ages,
    How do we know they are going to break?
There is no lull in the level firing,
    Nothing has shifted except the sun.
Yet we can feel they are tiring, tiring -
    Yet we can tell they are ripe to run.
Something wavers, and, while we wonder,
    Their centre-trenches are emptying out,
And, before their useless flanks go under,
    Our guns have pounded retreat to rout!

[1923]

The next poem, which seems to pre-figure the light touch of John Betjeman, notes how those who have gone through the harsh experiences of war at sea have to return to 'normal' life as if nothing had happened.

The Changelings

Sea Constables

(R.N.V.R.)

Or ever the battered liners sank
      With their passengers to the dark,
I was head of a Walworth Bank,
      And you were a grocer's clerk.

I was a dealer in stocks and shares,
      And you in butters and teas;
And we both abandoned our own affairs
      And took to the dreadful seas.

Wet and worry about our ways -
      Panic, onset and flight -
Had us in charge for a thousand days
      And a thousand-year-long night.

We saw more than the nights could hide -
      More than the waves could keep -
And - certain faces over the side
      Which do not go from our sleep.

We were more tired than words can tell
      While the pied craft fled by,
And the swinging mounds of the Western swell
      Hoisted us Heavens-high ...

Now there is nothing - not even our rank -
    To witness what we have been;
And I am returned to my Walworth Bank,
    And you to your margarine!

[1926]

Hymn of Breaking Strain *highlights the fact that, unlike materials, there is no way of calculating the breaking strain of men and women, who have to press on with their tasks despite past failures.*

It was designed to be sung to the tune of The Church's One Foundation.

Hymn of Breaking Strain

1935

The careful text books measure
      (Let all who build beware!)
The load, the shock, the pressure
      Material can bear.
So, when the buckled girder
      Lets down the grinding span,
The blame of loss, or murder,
      Is laid upon the man.
Not on the Stuff - the Man!

But in our daily dealing
      With stone and steel, we find
The Gods have no such feeling
      Of justice toward mankind.
To no set gauge they make us, -
      For no laid course prepare -
And presently o'ertake us
      With loads we cannot bear.
Too merciless to bear.

The prudent text-books give it
      In tables at the end -
The stress that shears a rivet
      Or makes a tie-bar bend -
What traffic wrecks macadam -
      What concrete should endure -

But we, poor Sons of Adam,
       Have no such literature,
To warn us or make sure!

We hold all Earth to plunder -
       All Time and Space as well -
Too wonder-stale to wonder
       At each new miracle;
Till, in mid-illusion
       Of Godhead 'neath our hand,
Falls multiple confusion
       On all we did or planned. -
The mighty works we planned.

We only of Creation
       (Oh, luckier bridge and rail!)
Abide the twin-damnation -
       To fail and know we fail.
Yet we - by which sole token
       We know we once were Gods -
Take shame in being broken
       However great the odds -
The Burden or the Odds.

Oh, veiled and secret Power
       Whose paths we seek in vain,
Be with us in our hour
       Of overthrow and pain;
That we - by which sure token
       We know thy ways are true -
In spite of being broken,
       Because of being broken,
May rise and build anew.
       Stand up and build anew!

Kipling had a restless urge to travel which he saw as the motive of the empire builder discovering and breaking new ground.

This stirring hymn to exploration was originally addressed to the poet's great friend, Wolcott Balestier. After Wolcott's death Kipling changed the words, 'dear lad' to 'dear lass' throughout, so as to make them refer to Wolcott's sister, Caroline, Kipling's bride to be.

L'Envoi

1892

There's a whisper down the field where the year has shot her yield,
     And the ricks stand grey to the sun,
Singing: - "Over then, come over, for the bee has quit the clover,
     And your English summer's done."
          You have heard the beat of the off-shore wind,
          And the thresh of the deep-sea rain;
          You have heard the song – how long? How long?
          Pull out on the trail again!
          Ha' done with the Tents of Shem, dear lass,
          We've seen the seasons through,
          And it's time to turn on the old trail, our own trail, the out trail,
          Pull out, pull out, on the Long Trail – the trail that is always new!

It's North you may run to the rime-ringed sun
     Or South to the blind Horn's hate;
Or East all the way into Mississippi Bay,
     Or West to the Golden Gate –
          Where the blindest bluffs hold good, dear lass,
          And the wildest tales are true,
          And the men bulk big on the old trail, our own trail, the out trail,
          And life runs large on the Long Trail – the trail that is always new.

The days are sick and cold, and the skies are grey and old
     And the twice-breathed airs blow damp;

200

And I'd sell my tired soul for the bucking beam-sea roll
    Of a black Bilbao tramp,
        With her load-line over her hatch, dear lass,
        And a drunken Dago crew,
        And her nose held down on the old trail, our own trail, the
        out trail
        From Cadiz south on the Long Trail – the trail that is al-
        ways new.

There be triple ways to take, of the eagle or the snake,
    Or the way of a man with a maid;
But the sweetest way to me is a Ship's upon the sea
    In the heel of the North-East Trade.
        Can you hear the crash on her brows, dear lass.
        And the drum of the racing screw,
        As she ships it green on the old trail, our own trail, the out
        trail,
        As she lifts and 'scends on the Long Trail – the trail that is
        always new?
See the shaking funnels roar, with the 'Peter at the fore,
And the fenders grind and heave,
And the derricks clack and grate, as the tackle hooks the crate,
    And the fall-rope whines through the sheave;
        It's "Gang-plank up and in," dear lass,
        It's "Hawsers warp her through!"
        And it's "All clear aft" on the old trail, our own trail, the
        out trail,
        We're backing down on the Long Trail – the trail that is
        always new.

Oh, the mutter overside, when the port-fog holds us tied,
    And the sirens hoot their dread,
When foot by foot we creep o'er the hueless, viewless deep
    To the sob of the questing lead!
        It's down by the Lower Hope, dear lass,
        With the Gunfleet Sands in view,

Till the Mouse swings green on the old trail, our own trail, the out trail,
And the Gull Light lifts on the Long Trail – the trail that is always new.

Oh the blazing tropic night, when the wake's a welt of light
    That holds the hot sky tame,
And the steady fore-foot snores through the planet-powdered floors
    Where the scared whale flukes in flame!
        Her plates are flaked by the sun, dear lass,
        And her ropes are taut with the dew,
        For we're booming down on the old trail, our own trail, the out trail,
        We're sagging south on the Long Trail – the trail that is always new.

Then home, get her home, where the drunken rollers comb,
    And the shouting seas drive by,
And the engines stamp and ring, and the wet bows reel and swing,
    And the Southern Cross rides high!
        Yes, the old lost stars wheel back, dear lass,
        That blaze in the velvet blue.
        They're all old friends on the old trail, our own trail, the out trail,
        They're God's own guides on the Long Trail – the trail that is always new.

Fly forward, O my heart, from the Foreland to the Start
    We're steaming all too slow,
And it's twenty thousand mile to our little lazy isle
    Where the trumpet-orchids blow!
        You have heard the call of the off-shore wind
        And the voice of the deep-sea rain;
        You have heard the song - how long? - How long?
        Pull out on the trail again!

The Lord knows what we may find, dear lass,
And The Deuce knows what we may do -
But we're back once more on the old trail, our own trail,
the out trail,
We're down, hull-down, on the Long Trail – the trail that
is always new!

For to Admire *is the song of a soldier reflecting soberly on the price he has to pay for his addiction to a life of travel.*

"For To Admire"

The Injian Ocean sets an' smiles
      So sof', so bright, so bloomin' blue;
There aren't a wave for miles an' miles
      Excep' the jiggle from the screw.
The ship is swep', the day is done,
      The bugle's gone for smoke and play;
An' black ag'in the settin' sun
      The Lascar sings, *"Hum deckty hai!"* [140]

For to admire an' for to see,
      For to be'old this world so wide --
It never done no good to me,
      But I can't drop it if I tried!

I see the Sergeants pitchin' quoits,
      I 'ear the women laugh an' talk,
I spy upon the quarter-deck
      The orficers an' lydies walk.
I thinks about the things that was,
      An' leans an' looks acrost the sea,
Till, spite of all the crowded ship
      There's no one lef' alive but me.

The things that was which I 'ave seen,
      In barrick, camp, an' action too,
I tells them over by myself,
      An' sometimes wonders if they're true;
For they was odd - most awful odd -
      But all the same, now they are o'er,

---

140 'I'm looking out'.

There must be 'eaps o' plenty such,
        An' if I wait I'll see some more.

Oh, I 'ave come upon the books,
        An' frequent broke a barrick-rule,
An' stood beside an' watched myself
        Be'avin' like a bloomin' fool.
I paid my price for findin' out,
        Nor never grutched the price I paid,
But sat in Clink without my boots,
        Admirin' 'ow the world was made.

Be'old a crowd upon the beam,
        An' 'umped above the sea appears
Old Aden, like a barrick-stove
        That no one's lit for years an' years.
I passed by that when I began,
        An' I go 'ome the road I came,
A time-expired soldier-man
        With six years' service to 'is name.

My girl she said, "Oh, stay with me!"
        My mother 'eld me to 'er breast.
They've never written none, an' so
        They must 'ave gone with all the rest -
With all the rest which I 'ave seen
        An' found an' known an' met along.
I cannot say the things I feel,
        And so I sing my evenin' song:

For to admire an' for to see,
        For to be'old this world so wide --
It never done no good to me,
        But I can't drop it if I tried.

[1894]

205

A sestina is a complex verse form of six stanzas invented by the mediaeval troubadours. To write such a poem in Cockney dialect in the space of only a few hours[141] was a remarkable achievement.

In substance it is a more optimistic piece than 'For to Admire'.

Sestina of the Tramp-Royal

1896

Speakin' in general, I 'ave tried 'em all,
The 'appy roads that take you o'er the world.
Speakin' in general, I 'ave found them good
For such as cannot use one bed too long,
But must get 'ence, the same as I 'ave done,
An' go observin' matters till they die.

What do it matter where or 'ow we die,
So long as we've our 'ealth to watch it all -
The different ways that different things are done,
An' men an' women lovin' in this world -
Takin' our chances as they come along,
An' when they ain't, pretendin' they are good?

In cash or credit - no, it aren't no good;
You 'ave to 'ave the 'abit or you'd die,
Unless you lived your life but one day long,
Nor didn't prophesy nor fret at all,
But drew your tucker some'ow from the world,
An' never bothered what you might ha' done.

But, Gawd, what things are they I 'aven't done?
I've turned my 'and to most, an' turned it good,
In various situations round the world -
For 'im that doth not work must surely die;

---

141 Carrington.

But that's no reason man should labour all
'Is life on one same shift; life's none so long.

Therefore, from job to job I've moved along.
Pay couldn't 'old me when my time was done,
For something in my 'ead upset me all,
Till I 'ad dropped whatever 'twas for good,
An', out at sea, be'eld the dock-lights die,
An' met my mate - the wind that tramps the world!

It's like a book, I think, this bloomin' world,
Which you can read and care for just so long,
But presently you feel that you will die
Unless you get the page you're readin' done,
An' turn another - likely not so good;
But what you're after is to turn 'em all.

Gawd bless this world! Whatever she 'ath done -
Excep' when awful long - I've found it good.
So write, before I die, "'E liked it all!"

The Explorer, *inspired perhaps by the opening up of Australia, is about the way some people are natural frontiersmen, driven to press ahead whatever the challenges.*

The Explorer

1898

"There's no sense in going further - it's the edge of cultivation,"
      So they said, and I believed it - broke my land and sowed my crop-
Built my barns and strung my fences in the little border station
      Tucked away below the foot hills where the trails run out and stop:

Till a voice, as bad as Conscience, rang interminable changes
      On one everlasting Whisper day and night repeated - so:
"Something hidden. Go and find it. Go and look behind the Ranges -
      "Something lost behind the Ranges. Lost and waiting for you.
Go!"

So I went, worn out of patience; never told my nearest neighbours -
      Stole away with pack and ponies – left 'em drinking in the town;
      And the faith that moveth mountains didn't seem to help my labours
      As I faced the sheer main-ranges, whipping up and leading down.

March by march I puzzled through 'em, turning flanks and dodging shoulders,
      Hurried on in hope of water, headed back for lack of grass;
Till I camped above the tree-line - drifted snow and naked boulders -
      Felt free air astir to windward - knew I'd stumbled on the Pass.

'Thought to name it for the finder: but that night the Norther found me -
      Froze and killed the plains-bred ponies; so I called the camp Despair

(It's the Railway Camp to-day, though). Then my Whisper waked to hound me: -

"Something lost behind the Ranges. Over yonder! Go you there!"

Then I knew, the while I doubted – knew His Hand was certain o'er me.
Still - it might be self-delusion - scores of better men had died -
I could reach the township living, but ... He knows what terrors tore me.
But I didn't ... but I didn't. I went down the other side.

Till the snow ran out in flowers, and the flowers turned to aloes,
And the aloes sprung to thickets and a brimming stream ran by;
But the thickets dwined to thorn-scrub, and the water drained to shallows -
And I dropped again on desert - blasted earth, and blasting sky ...

I remember lighting fires; I remember sitting by them;
I remember seeing faces, hearing voices through the smoke;
I remember they were fancy - for I threw a stone to try 'em.
"Something lost behind the Ranges" was the only word they spoke.

I remember going crazy. I remember that I knew it
When I heard myself hallooing to the funny folk I saw.
Very full of dreams that desert: but my two legs took me through it ...
And I used to watch' em moving with the toes all black and raw.

But at last the country altered - White Man's country past disputing -
Rolling grass and open timber, with a hint of hills behind -
There I found me food and water, and I lay a week recruiting,
Got my strength and lost my nightmares. Then I entered on my find.

Thence I ran my first rough survey - chose my trees and blazed and ringed 'em -
Week by week I pried and sampled - week by week my findings grew.

Saul he went to look for donkeys, and by God he found a kingdom!
  But by God, who sent His Whisper, I had struck the worth of two!

Up along the hostile mountains, where the hair-poised snowslide shivers -
  Down and through the big fat marshes that the virgin ore-bed
stains,
Till I heard the mile-wide mutterings of unimagined rivers,
  And beyond the nameless timber saw illimitable plains!

Plotted sites of future cities, traced the easy grades between 'em;
  Watched unharnessed rapids wasting fifty thousand head an
hour;
Counted leagues of water-frontage through the axe-ripe woods that
screen 'em -
  Saw the plant to feed a people - up and waiting for the power!

Well I know who'll take the credit - all the clever chaps that followed -
  Came, a dozen men together - never knew my desert fears;
Tracked me by the camps I'd quitted, used the water-holes I'd hollowed.
  They'll go back and do the talking. *They'll* be called the Pioneers!

They will find my sites of townships - not the cities that I set there.
  They will rediscover rivers - not my rivers heard at night.
By my own old marks and bearings they will show me how to get there,
  By the lonely cairns I builded they will guide my feet aright.

Have I named one single river? Have I claimed one single acre?
  Have I kept one single nugget - (barring samples)? No, not I!
Because my price was paid me ten times over by my Maker.
  But you wouldn't understand it. You go up and occupy.

Ores you'll find there; wood and cattle; water-transit sure and steady
  (That should keep the railway rates down), coal and iron at your
doors.

God took care to hide the country till He judged His people ready,
    Then He chose me for His Whisper, and I've found it, and it's
yours!

Yes, your "Never-never country" - yes, your "edge of cultivation"
    And "no sense in going further" - till I crossed the range to see.
God forgive me! No, I didn't. It's God's present to our nation.
    Anybody might have found it but - His Whisper came to me!

ENGLAND

Rather like GK Chesterton's character, who, after travelling the whole world round, discovered a beautiful, magical country which turned out to be his own, so Kipling, after a life spent roaming, discovered in England the place he was to make his final home. As he explains in the last stanza of his poem, *Sussex*:

> God gives all men all earth to love,
> But since man's heart is small,
> Ordains for each one spot shall prove
> Beloved over all.
> Each to his choice, and I rejoice
> The lot has fallen to me
> In a fair ground - in a fair ground -
> Yea, Sussex by the sea!

Every nation has its share of men forced to leave their native land in order to avoid legal or other ignominy. Kipling acknowledged their plight in the following poem The title influenced T.S. Eliot when he came to write The Hollow Men.

The poem referred to Callao in Peru which Kipling had just visited. The Lord Warden is both the guardian of the Cinque Ports and the name of a famous pub in Dover.

The Broken Men

1902

For things we never mention,
    For Art misunderstood -
For excellent intention
    That did not turn to good;
From ancient tales' renewing,
    From clouds we would not clear -
Beyond the Law's pursuing
    We fled, and settled here.

We took no tearful leaving,
    We bade no long good-byes.
Men talked of crime and thieving,
    Men wrote of fraud and lies.
To save our injured feelings
    'Twas time and time to go -
Behind was dock and Dartmoor,
    Ahead lay Callao!

The widow and the orphan
    That pray for ten per cent,
They clapped their trailers on us
    To spy the road we went.
They watched the foreign sailings
    (They scan the shipping still),

And that's your Christian people
     Returning good for ill!

God bless the thoughtful islands
     Where never warrants come;
God bless the just Republics
     That give a man a home,
That ask no foolish questions,
     But set him on his feet;
And save his wife and daughters
     From the workhouse and the street!

On church and square and market
     The noonday silence falls;
You'll hear the drowsy mutter
     Of the fountain in our halls.
Asleep amid the yuccas
     The city takes her ease -
Till twilight brings the land-wind
     To the clicking jalousies.

Day long the diamond weather,
     The high, unaltered blue -
The smell of goats and incense
     And the mule-bells tinkling through.
Day long the warder ocean
     That keeps us from our kin,
And once a month our levee
     When the English mail comes in.

You'll find us up and waiting
     To treat you at the bar;
You'll find us less exclusive
     Than the average English are.
We'll meet you with a carriage,
     Too glad to show you round,

But - we do not lunch on steamers,
       For they are English ground.

We sail o' nights to England
       And join our smiling Boards -
Our wives go in with Viscounts
       And our daughters dance with Lords,
But behind our princely doings,
       And behind each coup we make,
We feel there's Something Waiting,
       And - we meet It when we wake.

Ah, God! One sniff of England -
       To greet our flesh and blood -
To hear the traffic slurring
       Once more through London mud!
Our towns of wasted honour -
       Our streets of lost delight!
How stands the old Lord Warden?
       Are Dover's cliffs still white?

Puck's song, *which needs no commentary, is an evocation of the living past around the poet's Sussex home, Bateman's. Like so many of the poems in this anthology it came from his collection of short stories,* Puck of Pook's Hill.

Puck's Song

See you the ferny ride that steals
Into the oak-woods far?
Oh, that was whence they hewed the keels
That rolled to Trafalgar!

And mark you where the ivy clings
To Bayham's mouldering walls?
Oh there we cast the stout railings
That stand around St. Paul's!

See you the dimpled track that runs
All hollow through the wheat?
Oh that was where they hauled the guns
That smote King Philip's fleet!

(Out of the Weald, the secret Weald,
Men sent in ancient years,
The horse-shoes red at Flodden Field,
The arrows at Poitiers!)

See you our little mill that clacks,
So busy by the brook?
She has ground her corn and paid her tax
Ever since Domesday Book.

See you our stilly woods of oak,
And the dread ditch beside?
Oh, that was where the Saxons broke
On the day that Harold died!

See you the windy levels spread
About the gates of Rye?
Oh, that was where the Northmen fled,
When Alfred's ships came by!

See you our pastures wide and lone,
 Where the red oxen browse?
Oh, there was a City thronged and known,
 Ere London boasted a house!

And see you, after rain, the trace
Of mound and ditch and wall?
 Oh that was a Legion's camping-place,
When Caesar sailed from Gaul!

And see you marks that show and fade,
 Like shadows on the Downs?
Oh they are the lines the Flint Men made,
 To guard their wondrous towns!

Trackway and Camp and City lost,
 Salt Marsh where now is corn-
Old Wars, old Peace, old Arts that cease,
And so was England born!

She is not any common Earth,
Water or wood or air,
But Merlin's Isle of Gramarye,
 Where you and I will fare!

[1906]

Written as an introductory poem for C.R.L. Fletcher's A School History of England, The River's Tale *is a fair example of the poet's ability to use simple language to captivate the mind of child and man alike.*

The river, of course, is the Thames.

The River's Tale

(Prehistoric)

> Twenty bridges from Tower to Kew -
> Wanted to know what the River knew,
> (Twenty bridges or twenty-two,)
> For they were young, and the Thames was old
> And this is the tale that the River told:-

I walk my beat before London Town,
Five hours up and seven down.
Up I go till I end my run
At Tide-end-town, which is Teddington.
Down I come with the mud in my hands
And plaster it over the Maplin Sands.
But I'd have you know that these waters of mine
Were once a branch of the River Rhine,
When hundreds of miles to the East I went
And England was joined to the Continent.
I remember the bat-winged lizard-birds,
The Age of Ice and the mammoth herds,
And the Giant Tigers that stalked them down
Through Regent's Park into Camden Town.
And I remember like yesterday
The earliest Cockney who came my way,
When he pushed through the forest that lined the Strand,
With paint on his face and a club in his hand.
He was death to feather and fin and fur.
He trapped my beavers at Westminster.

He netted my salmon, he hunted my deer,
He killed my heron off Lambeth Pier.
He fought his neighbour with axes and swords,
Flint or bronze, at my upper fords,
While down at Greenwich, for slaves and tin,
The tall Phoenician ships stole in,
And North Sea war-boats, painted and gay,
Flashed like dragon-flies, Erith way;
And Norseman and Negro and Gaul and Greek
Drank with the Britons in Barking Creek,
And life was gay, and the world was new,
And I was a mile across at Kew!
But the Roman came with a heavy hand,
And bridged and roaded and ruled the land,
And the Roman left and the Danes blew in -
And that's where your history-books begin!

[1911]

STORYTELLING

Kipling was a storyteller *par excellence* in prose or verse. Here are a few of his narrative poems.

The following story in ballad form about a mother's twofold loss is, in the words of the Kipling Society New Readers' Guide, 'an amazing piece from a young unmarried man.' The terse language is effective, if unusual, for the poet.

The Gift of the Sea

1890

The dead child lay in the shroud,
  And the widow watched beside;
And her mother slept, and the Channel swept
  The gale in the teeth of the tide.

But the mother laughed at all.
  "I have lost my man in the sea,
And the child is dead. Be still," she said,
  "What more can ye do to me?"

The widow watched the dead,
  And the candle guttered low,
And she tried to sing the Passing Song
  That bids the poor soul go.

And "Mary take you now," she sang,
  "That lay against my heart."
And "Mary smooth your crib to-night,"
  But she could not say "Depart."

Then came a cry from the sea,
  But the sea-rime blinded the glass,
And "Heard ye nothing, mother?" she said,
  "'Tis the child that waits to pass."

And the nodding mother sighed.
  "'Tis a lambing ewe in the whin,

"For why should the christened soul cry out
        "That never knew of sin?"

"O feet I have held in my hand,
        O hands at my heart to catch,
How should they know the road to go,
        And how should they lift the latch?"

They laid a sheet to the door,
        With the little quilt atop,
That it might not hurt from the cold or the dirt,
        But the crying would not stop.

The widow lifted the latch
        And strained her eyes to see,
And opened the door on the bitter shore
        To let the soul go free.

There was neither glimmer nor ghost,
        There was neither spirit nor spark,
And "Heard ye nothing, mother?" she said,
        "'Tis crying for me in the dark."

And the nodding mother sighed:
        "'Tis sorrow makes ye dull;
Have ye yet to learn the cry of the tern,
        Or the wail of the wind-blown gull?"

"The terns are blown inland,
        The gray gull follows the plough.
'Twas never a bird, the voice I heard,
        O mother, I hear it now!"

"Lie still, dear lamb, lie still;
        The child is passed from harm,
'Tis the ache in your breast that broke your rest,
        And the feel of an empty arm."

She put her mother aside,
      "In Mary's name let be!
For the peace of my soul I must go," she said,
      And she went to the calling sea.

In the heel of the wind-bit pier,
      Where the twisted weed was piled,
She came to the life she had missed by an hour,
      For she came to a little child.

She laid it into her breast,
      And back to her mother she came,
But it would not feed and it would not heed,
      Though she gave it her own child's name.

And the dead child dripped on her breast,
      And her own in the shroud lay stark;
And "God forgive us, mother," she said,
      "We let it die in the dark!"

The following lines were written by one of the characters in Kipling's tale,
The Finest Story in the World. *Composed in bed, they are described as be-*
ing 'centipede metres', that is metres with too many feet. It is a rare, but
outstandingly successful, example of Kipling's use of rhymed, but otherwise
free verse. Note the increasing length of the lines.

Song of the Galley-slaves

We pulled for you when the wind was against us and the sails were low. -
Will you never let us go?
We ate bread and onions when you took towns, or ran aboard quickly
when you were beaten back by the foe
The Captains walked up and down the deck in fair weather singing songs,
but we were below.
We fainted with our chins on the oars and you did not see that we were
idle for we still swung to and fro.
Will you never let us go?
The salt made the oar-handles like shark-skin; our knees were cut to the
bone with salt-cracks; our hair was stuck to our foreheads; and our lips
were cut to our gums, and you whipped us because we could not row.
Will you never let us go?
But in a little time we shall run out of the portholes as the water runs
along the oar-blade, and though you tell the others to row after us you
will never catch us till you catch the oar-thresh and tie up the winds in
the belly of the sail. Aho!
Will you never let us go?

[1891]

The following 'terrifying vision of doom', as Prof. Dobrée called it, first appeared as chapter headings in Kipling's novel, The Light that Failed. *Pulled together, the verses are greater than their parts.*

'Hirples' means limps.

Heriot's Ford

"What's that that hirples at my side?"
The foe that you must fight, my lord.
"That rides as fast as I can ride?"
The shadow of your might, my lord.

"Then wheel my horse against the foe!"
He's down and overpast, my lord.
You war against the sunset-glow,
The judgment follows fast, my lord.

"Oh who will stay the sun's descent?"
King Joshua he is dead, my lord.
"I need an hour to repent!"
'Tis what our sister said, my lord.

"Oh do not slay me in my sins!"
You're safe awhile with us, my lord.
"Nay, kill me ere my fear begins."
We would not serve you thus, my lord.

"Where is the doom that I must face?"
Three little leagues away, my lord.
"Then mend the horses' laggard pace!"
We need them for next day, my lord.

"Next day - next day! Unloose my cords!"
Our sister needed none, my lord.
You had no mind to face our swords,
And - where can cowards run, my lord?

"You would not kill the soul alive?"
'Twas thus our sister cried, my lord.
"I dare not die with none to shrive."
But so our sister died, my lord.

"Then wipe the sweat from brow and cheek."
It runnels forth afresh, my lord.
"Uphold me - for the flesh is weak."
You've finished with the Flesh, my lord.

[1891]

This ballad, though it has been set to music more than once, is as far removed from the popular concept of a sailor's shanty as you can get.

It is an allegory of early religion, in which a man takes a woman from her tribe, who set off in pursuit. The couple - for that is what they have become - escape and, after enduring a test of some sort, return as 'prophet and priestess'.

The First Chantey

1896

Mine was the woman to me, darkling I found her;
Haling her dumb from the camp, took her and bound her.
Hot rose her Tribe on our track ere I had proved her;
Hearing her laugh in the gloom, greatly I loved her.

Swift through the forest we ran, none stood to guard us,
Few were my people and far; then the flood barred us -
Him we call Son of the Sea, sullen and swollen.
Panting we waited the death, stealer and stolen.

Yet ere they came to my lance laid for the slaughter,
Lightly she leaped to a log lapped in the water;
Holding on high and apart skins that arrayed her,
Called she the God of the Wind that He should aid her.

Life had the tree at that word (Praise we the Giver!)
Otter-like left he the bank for the full river.
Far fell their axes behind, flashing and ringing,
Wonder was on me and fear - yet she was singing!

Low lay the land we had left. Now the blue bound us,
Even the Floor of the Gods level around us.
Whisper there was not, nor word, shadow nor showing,
Till the light stirred on the deep, glowing and growing.

228

Then did He leap to His place flaring from under,
He the Compeller, the Sun, bared to our wonder.
Nay, not a league from our eyes blinded with gazing,
Cleared He the gate of the world, huge and amazing!

This we beheld (and we live) - the Pit of the Burning!
Then the God spoke to the tree for our returning;
Back to the beach of our flight, fearless and slowly,
Back to our slayers went he: but we were holy.

Men that were hot in that hunt, women that followed,
Babes that were promised our bones, trembled and wallowed!
Over the necks of the Tribe crouching and fawning -
Prophet and priestess we came back from the dawning!

The Truce of the Bear *was intended by the author to be read as a metaphor of Russia's imperial ambitions in Asia. However, it reads equally well as a straightforward story of hunter and hunted, and how the roles can all too easily be reversed.*

The Truce of the Bear

1898

Yearly, with tent and rifle, our careless white men go
By the Pass called Muttianee, to shoot in the vale below.
Yearly by Muttianee he follows our white men in -
Matun, the old blind beggar, bandaged from brow to chin.

Eyeless, noseless, and lipless - toothless, broken of speech,
Seeking a dole at the doorway he mumbles his tale to each;
Over and over the story, ending as he began:
"Make ye no truce with Adam-zad - the Bear that walks like a Man!

There was a flint in my musket - pricked and primed was the pan,
When I went hunting Adam-zad - the Bear that stands like a Man.
I looked my last on the timber, I looked my last on the snow,
When I went hunting Adam-zad fifty summers ago!

I knew his times and his seasons, as he knew mine, that fed
By night in the ripened maizefield and robbed my house of bread.
I knew his strength and cunning, as he knew mine, that crept
At dawn to the crowded goat-pens and plundered while I slept.

Up from his stony playground - down from his well-digged lair -
Out on the naked ridges ran Adam-zad the Bear -
Groaning, grunting, and roaring, heavy with stolen meals,
Two long marches to northward, and I was at his heels!

Two full marches to northward, at the fall of the second night,
I came on mine enemy Adam-zad all panting from his flight.

There was a charge in the musket - pricked and primed was the pan -
My finger crooked on the trigger - when he reared up like a man.

Horrible, hairy, human, with paws like hands in prayer,
Making his supplication rose Adam-zad the Bear.
I looked at the swaying shoulders, at the paunch's swag and swing,
And my heart was touched with pity for the monstrous, pleading thing.

"Touched with pity and wonder, I did not fire then ...
I have looked no more on women - I have walked no more with men.
Nearer he tottered and nearer, with paws like hands that pray -
From brow to jaw that steel-shod paw, it ripped my face away!

Sudden, silent, and savage, searing as flame the blow -
Faceless I fell before his feet, fifty summers ago.
I heard him grunt and chuckle - I heard him pass to his den.
He left me blind to the darkened years and the little mercy of men.

"Now ye go down in the morning with guns of the newer style,
That load (I have felt) in the middle and range (I have heard) a mile?
Luck to the white man's rifle, that shoots so fast and true,
But - pay, and I lift my bandage and show what the Bear can do!"

(Flesh like slag in the furnace, knobbed and withered and grey -
Matun, the old blind beggar, he gives good worth for his pay.)
"Rouse him at noon in the bushes, follow and press him hard -
Not for his ragings and roarings flinch ye from Adam-zad.

But (pay, and I put back the bandage) *this* is the time to fear,
When he stands up like a tired man, tottering near and near;
When he stands up as pleading, in wavering, man-brute guise,
When he veils the hate and cunning of his little, swinish eyes;

When he shows as seeking quarter, with paws like hands in prayer
That is the time of peril - the time of the Truce of the Bear!"

Eyeless, noseless, and lipless, asking a dole at the door,
Matun, the old blind beggar, he tells it o'er and o'er;
Fumbling and feeling the rifles, warming his hands at the flame,
Hearing our careless white men talk of the morrow's game;

Over and over the story, ending as he began: -
"There is no truce with Adam-zad, the Bear that looks like a Man!"

The parable of the prodigal son (Luke XV, 11-32) is the tale of a father who divides his inheritance between his two sons. The older invests it wisely, while the younger spends it on 'prodigal living' and loose women. When famine comes, the younger son finds himself reduced to tending swine (a tainted food for Jews) and decides to cast himself on his father's mercy. Delighted to have him back, the father gives him his best robe and kills the fatted calf for a celebratory meal. Hearing the sounds of merriment, the older son complains he has been badly done by. His father thinks it sufficient to reply: 'It was right that we should make merry and be glad, for your brother was dead and is alive again, and was lost and is found.'

Luke does not tell us what the older son thought of this.

In Kipling's jaunty paraphrase of the Bible story the action is removed to the poet's day when the younger son boasts of the skill he has acquired in the rearing of hogs in what seem to be the Chicago stock-yards. Never really repentant, even in the original version, the younger son is now frankly cynical about his actions and happy to reveal just what he thinks of his family.

Kipling skilfully uses a triple rhyme to begin each stanza.

The Prodigal Son

(Western Version)

Here come I to my own again,
Fed, forgiven and known again,
Claimed by bone of my bone again
And cheered by flesh of my flesh.
The fatted calf is dressed for me,
But the husks have greater zest for me,
I think my pigs will be best for me,
So I'm off to the Yards afresh.

I never was very refined, you see,
(And it weighs on my brother's mind, you see)
But there's no reproach among swine, d'you see,

For being a bit of a swine.
So I'm off with wallet and staff to eat
The bread that is three parts chaff to wheat,
But glory be! - there's a laugh to it,
Which isn't the case when we dine.

My father glooms and advises me,
My brother sulks and despises me,
And Mother catechises me
Till I want to go out and swear.
And, in spite of the butler's gravity,
I know that the servants have it I
Am a monster of moral depravity,
And I'm damned if I think it's fair!

I wasted my substance, I know I did,
On riotous living, so I did,
But there's nothing on record to show I did
Worse than my betters have done.
They talk of the money I spent out there -
They hint at the pace that I went out there -
But they all forget I was sent out there
Alone as a rich man's son.

So I was a mark for plunder at once,
And lost my cash (can you wonder?) at once,
But I didn't give up and knock under at once,
I worked in the Yards, for a spell,
Where I spent my nights and my days with hogs.
And shared their milk and maize with hogs,
Till, I guess, I have learned what pays with hogs
And - I have that knowledge to sell!

So back I go to my job again,
Not so easy to rob again,
Nor quite so ready to sob again
On any neck that's around.

I'm leaving, Pater. Good-bye to you!
God bless you, Mater! I'll write to you ...
I wouldn't be impolite to you,
But, Brother, you are a hound!

[1901]

Though written for children, The Looking Glass *has a disturbing air of menace. The Poet Laureate, Robert Bridges described it as 'masterful' and having 'an irresistible force'.*[142] *Did Kipling, I wonder, have Elizabeth's distressing death in mind when he wrote it?*

The Looking Glass

(A Country Dance)

Queen Bess was Harry's daughter. (Stand forward partners all!)
In ruff and stomacher and gown
She danced King Philip down-a-down,
And left her shoe to show 'twas true,
        (The very tune I'm playing you)
In Norgem at Brickwall!

The Queen was in her chamber, and she was middling old,
Her petticoat was satin, and her stomacher was gold.
Backward and forward and sideways did she pass,
Making up her mind to face the cruel looking-glass.
 The cruel looking-glass that will never show a lass
 As comely or as kindly or as young as what she was!

 Queen Bess was Harry's daughter. (Now hand your partners all!)

The Queen was in her chamber, a-combing of her hair.
There came Queen Mary's spirit and It stood behind her chair,
Singing "Backward and forward and sideways may you pass,
 But I will stand behind you till you face the looking-glass.
The cruel looking-glass that will never show a lass
As lovely or unlucky or as lonely as I was!"

Queen Bess was Harry's daughter. (Now turn your partners all!)

---

142 *Collected Essays of Robert Bridges* XIII, Oxford, 1933.

The Queen was in her chamber, a-weeping very sore,
There came Lord Leicester's spirit and It scratched upon the door,
Singing "Backward and forward and sideways may you pass,
But I will walk beside you till you face the looking-glass.
The cruel looking-glass that will never show a lass,
As hard and unforgiving or as wicked as you was!"

Queen Bess was Harry's daughter. (Now kiss your partners all!)

The Queen was in her chamber, her sins were on her head.
She looked the spirits up and down and statelily she said:,
"Backward and forward and sideways though I've been,
Yet I am Harry's daughter and I am England's Queen!"
And she faced the looking-glass (and whatever else there was)
And she saw her day was over and she saw her beauty pass
In the cruel looking-glass, that can always hurt a lass
More hard than any ghost there is or any man there was!

[1909]

A St Helena Lullaby *is a conversation between Napoleon and an unidentified narrator. It concerns the last six years of the emperor's life as a prisoner of the British on the bleak Atlantic island of St Helena. The poem was described by Angus Wilson as characteristic of Kipling's 'dark and cautious pessimism'. The present editor prefers to view it as a haunting song of nemesis.*

A St. Helena Lullaby

"How far is St. Helena from a little child at play!"
What makes you want to wander there with all the world between?
Oh, Mother, call your son again or else he'll run away.
(No one thinks of winter when the grass is green!)

"How far is St. Helena from a fight in Paris street?"
I haven't time to answer now - the men are falling fast.
The guns begin to thunder, and the drums begin to beat.
(If you take the first step, you will take the last!)

"How far is St. Helena from the field of Austerlitz?"
You couldn't hear me if I told - so loud the cannons roar.
But not so far for people who are living by their wits.
("Gay go up" means "Gay go down" the wide world o'er!)

"How far is St. Helena from the Emperor of France."
I cannot see - I cannot tell - the Crowns they dazzle so.
The Kings sit down to dinner, and the Queens stand up to dance.
(After open weather you may look for snow!)

"How far is St. Helena from the Capes of Trafalgar?"
A longish way – longish way - with ten more to run.
It's South across the water underneath a falling star.
(What you cannot finish you must leave undone!)

"How far is St. Helena from the Beresina ice?"
An ill way - a chill way - the ice begins to crack.
But not so far for gentlemen who never took advice.
(*When you can't go forward you must e'en come back!*)

"How far is St. Helena from the field of Waterloo?"
A near way - a clear way - the ship will take you soon.
A pleasant place for gentlemen with little left to do.
(*Morning never tries you till the afternoon!*)

"How far from St. Helena to the Gate of Heaven's Grace?"
That no one knows - that no one knows - and no one ever will.
But fold your hands across your heart and cover up your face,
And after all your trapesings, child, lie still!

[1910]

The next piece of unrhymed verse is based on the conceit that Shakespeare's method of working owed more to practical example than romantic imagination. In form it owes much to the Roman poet, Horace.

But why is the Bard supposed to believe his works to be 'shows of no earthly importance'?

The Craftsman

Once, after long-drawn revel at The Mermaid,
He to the overbearing Boanerges
Jonson, uttered (if half of it were liquor,
         Blessed be the vintage!)

Saying how, at an alehouse under Cotswold,
He had made sure of his very Cleopatra,
Drunk with enormous, salvation-contemning
         Love for a tinker.

How, while he hid from Sir Thomas's keepers,
Crouched in a ditch and drenched by the midnight
Dews, he had listened to gipsy Juliet
         Rail at the dawning.

How at Bankside, a boy drowning kittens
Winced at the business; whereupon his sister -
Lady Macbeth aged seven - thrust 'em under,
         Sombrely scornful.

How on a Sabbath, hushed and compassionate -
She being known since her birth to the townsfolk -
Stratford dredged and delivered from Avon
         Dripping Ophelia.

So, with a thin third finger marrying
Drop to wine-drop domed on the table,
Shakespeare opened his heart till the sunrise
       Entered to hear him.

London waked and he, imperturbable,
Passed from waking to hurry after shadows ...
Busied upon shows of no earthly importance?
       Yes, but he knew it!

[1919]

THE GREATHEARTED

This section draws together some of the poet's nobler aspirations which do not fall readily within any of the preceding themes.

The proud mothers in the maternity hospital love, obey, but secretly smile at the young sister in charge of them who 'hath no breasts' because she is still 'a field untilled, a web unwove'.

This expression of mutual love and trust demonstrates the ability, often observed by the poet, of people to hold mutually conflicting roles at the same time.

The Nursing Sister

(Maternity Hospital)

Our sister sayeth such and such,
And we must bow to her behests;
Our sister toileth overmuch,
Our little maid that hath no breasts.

A field untilled, a web unwove,
A flower withheld from sun or bee,
An alien in the Courts of Love,
And - teacher unto such as we!

We love her, but we laugh the while,
We laugh, but sobs are mixed with laughter;
Our sister hath no time to smile,
She knows not what must follow after.

Wind of the South, arise and blow,
From beds of spice thy locks shake free;
Breathe on her heart that she may know,
Breathe on her eyes that she may see!

Alas! we vex her with our mirth,
And maze her with most tender scorn,
Who stands beside the Gates of Birth,
Herself a child - a child unborn!

Our sister sayeth such and such,
And we must bow to her behests;
Our sister toileth overmuch,
Our little maid that hath no breasts.

[1892]

In The Captive *Kipling shows how a slave may be an example to his captors. It was published as an epigraph to the short story of the same name in his collection,* Traffics and Discoveries.

It appears to be spoken by an Arab, the race who were the originators and exploiters of the slave trade.

The Captive

Not with an outcry to Allah nor any complaining
He answered his name at the muster and stood to the chaining.
When the twin anklets were nipped on the leg-bars that held them,
He brotherly greeted the armourers stooping to weld them.
Ere the sad dust of the marshalled feet of the chain-gang swallowed him,
Observing him nobly at ease, I alighted and followed him.
Thus we had speech by the way, but not touching his sorrow -
Rather his red Yesterday and his regal To-morrow,
Wherein he statelily moved to the clink of his chains unregarded,
Nowise abashed but contented to drink of the potion awarded.
Saluting aloofly his Fate, he made haste with his story,
And the words of his mouth were as slaves spreading carpets of glory
Embroidered with names of the Djinns - a miraculous weaving -
But the cool and perspicuous eye overbore unbelieving.
So I submitted myself to the limits of rapture -
Bound by this man we had bound, amid captives his capture -
Till he returned me to earth and the visions departed.
But on him be the Peace and the Blessing; for he was greathearted!

[1903]

Jobson's Amen was based on the experience of the contingent of Gurkhas who formed the ceremonial guard for the lying in state of King Edward VII. Its message needs no comment from the editor.

The Kipling Society's New Reader's Guide suggests that the title may have been based on Hobson-Jobson, the Anglo-Indian dictionary.

Jobson's Amen

In the Presence

"Blessèd be the English and all their ways and works.
Cursed be the Infidels, Hereticks, and Turks!"
"Amen," quo' Jobson, "But where I used to lie
Was neither Candle, Bell nor Book to curse my brethren by,

"But a palm-tree in full bearing, bowing down, bowing down,
To a surf that drove unsparing at the brown, walled town,
Conches in a temple, oil-lamps in a dome,
And a low moon out of Africa said: 'This way home!'"

"Blessèd be the English and all that they profess.
Cursèd be the Savages that prance in nakedness!"
"Amen," quo' Jobson, "but where I used to lie
Was neither shirt nor pantaloons to catch my brethren by:

"But a well-wheel slowly creaking, going round, going round,
By a water-channel leaking over drowned, warm ground,
Parrots very busy in the trellised pepper-vine,
And a high sun over Asia shouting: 'Rise and shine!'"

"Blessèd be the English and everything they own.
Cursèd be the Infidels that bow to wood and stone!"
"Amen," quo' Jobson, "but where I used to lie
Was neither pew nor Gospelleer to save my brethren by:

"But a desert stretched and stricken, left and right, left and right,
Where the piled mirages thicken under white-hot light -
A skull beneath a sand-hill and a viper coiled inside,
And a red wind out of Libya roaring: 'Run and hide!'"

"Blessèd be the English and all they make or do.
Cursèd be the Hereticks who doubt that this is true!"
"Amen," quo' Jobson, "but where I mean to die
Is neither rule nor calliper to judge the matter by:

"But Himalaya heavenward-heading, sheer and vast, sheer and vast,
In a million summits bedding on the last world's past -
A certain sacred mountain where the scented cedars climb,
And, the feet of my Beloved hurrying back through Time!"

[1914]

In We and They, *Kipling makes the same point as in Jobson's Amen, but somewhat more light-heartedly and in an English, as opposed to an Indian, context.*

We and They

A Friend of the Family

Father, Mother, and Me
      Sister and Auntie say
All the people like us are We,
      And every one else is They.
And They live over the sea,
      While We live over the way,
But - would you believe it? – They look upon We
      As only a sort of They!

We eat pork and beef
      With cow-horn-handled knives.
They who gobble Their rice off a leaf,
      Are horrified out of Their lives;
And They who live up a tree,
      And feast on grubs and clay,
(Isn't it scandalous?) look upon We
      As a simply disgusting They!

We shoot birds with a gun.
      They stick lions with spears.
Their full-dress is un-.
      We dress up to Our ears.
They like Their friends for tea.
      We like Our friends to stay;
And, after all that,
      They look upon We
As an utterly ignorant They!

We eat kitcheny food.
     We have doors that latch.
They drink milk or blood,
     Under an open thatch.
We have Doctors to fee.
     They have Wizards to pay.
And (impudent heathen!) They look upon We
     As a quite impossible They!

All good people agree,
     And all good people say,
All nice people, like Us, are We
     And every one else is They:
But if you cross over the sea,
     Instead of over the way,
You may end by (think of it!) looking on We
     As only a sort of They!

[1914]

The Aberdeen Terrier-loving Kipling knew that Man has few friends as faithful as a dog. His most well known poem on the subject is The Power of the Dog, *but the present editor finds the following piece more moving.*

"His Apologies"

1932

Master, this is Thy Servant. He is rising eight weeks old.
He is mainly Head and Tummy. His legs are uncontrolled.
But Thou hast forgiven his ugliness, and settled him on Thy knee ...
Art Thou content with Thy Servant? He is *very* comfy with Thee.

Master, behold a Sinner! He hath committed a wrong.
He hath defiled Thy Premises through being kept in too long.
Wherefore his nose has been rubbed in the dirt and his self- respect has been bruiséd.
Master, pardon Thy Sinner, and see he is properly loosed.

Master, again Thy Sinner! This that was once Thy Shoe,
He has found and taken and carried aside, as fitting matter to chew.
Now there is neither blacking nor tongue, and the Housemaid has us in tow.
Master, remember Thy Servant is young, and tell her to let him go!

Master, extol Thy Servant, he has met a most Worthy Foe!
There has been fighting all over the Shop - and into the Shop also!
Till cruel umbrellas parted the strife (or I might have been choking him yet),
But Thy Servant has had the Time of his Life -- and now shall we call on the vet?

Master, behold Thy Servant! Strange children came to play,
And because they fought to caress him, Thy Servant wentedst away.
But now that the Little Beasts have gone, he has returned to see
(Brushed - with his Sunday collar on) what they left over from tea.
....

251

Master, pity Thy Servant! He is deaf and three parts blind.
He cannot catch Thy Commandments. He cannot read Thy Mind.
Oh, leave him not to his loneliness; nor make him that kitten's scorn.
He hath had no other God than Thee since the year that he was born.

Lord, look down on Thy Servant! Bad things have come to pass.
There is no heat in the midday sun, nor health in the wayside grass.
His bones are full of an old disease - his torments run and increase.
Lord, make haste with Thy Lightnings and grant him a quick release!

FAITH AND THE NUMINOUS

Like Shakespeare, Kipling's religious views, if any, remain elusive. Both his parents were born into the devout Methodist tradition, but had lapsed. Their son's references to the Bible and the Collects (which he was forced to read as a child in 'The House of Desolation') should not be taken as evidence of conformity to any orthodoxy.

Philip Mason wrote that Kipling, while 'Faithful to an unknown God, ... was agnostic about formulations.' Like many doubters, he did not find it necessary to resort to dogma to explain fundamental spiritual values such as atonement, forgiveness, compassion and the redemptive power of suffering, all of which he returned to again and again. He realized that, if there is a divinity, it must be ineffable, something which the mind of man is too puny to comprehend. In one of his poems he prayed for,

> A veil 'twixt us and Thee, Good Lord,
> A veil 'twixt us and Thee,
> Lest we should hear too clear, too clear,
> And unto madness see![143]

---

143 *The Prayer of Miriam Cohen.*

Kipling wrote six poems in the style of an 'envois', or concluding poetic remarks. The first, composed while he was still a young man, is a short but arresting piece in which an observer poignantly describes how the believers were 'betrayed' by their god, but nevertheless yearn for its return.

L'Envoi

To whom it may concern

The smoke upon your altar dies,
    The flowers decay.
The Goddess of your sacrifice
    Has flown away.
What profit then to sing or slay
The sacrifice from day to day?

"We know the Shrine is void," they said,
    The Goddess flown -
Yet wreaths are on the altar laid -
    The Altar-Stone
Is black with fumes of sacrifice,
Albeit She has fled our eyes.

For, it may be, if still we sing
    And tend the Shrine,
Some deity on wandering wing
    May there incline;
And finding all in order meet,
Stay while we worship at Her feet."

[1886]

The next poem tells the story of a stone consigned to utter darkness by the apparent caprice of fate, and questions why, without fault, the stone should be so punished. The sentiment is reminiscent of Islamic fatalism.

Kipling returned to the same theme in his poem, The Answer *(not included).*

"By the Hoof of the Wild Goat"

By the Hoof of the Wild Goat uptossed
From the Cliff where she lay in the Sun
Fell the Stone
To the Tarn where the daylight is lost,
So she fell from the light of the Sun
And alone!

Now the fall was ordained from the first
With the Goat and the Cliff and the Tarn,
But the Stone
Knows only her life is accursed
As she sinks from the light of the Sun,
And alone!

Oh Thou Who hast builded the World,
Oh Thou Who hast lighted the Sun,
Oh Thou Who hast darkened the Tarn,
Judge Thou
The sin of the Stone that was hurled
By the goat from the light of the Sun,
As she sinks in the mire of the Tarn,
Even now - even now - even now!

[1888]

The next envoi *has been described on good authority as 'in effect' a Masonic prayer.*[144] *Kipling was, indeed, proud to be a Mason, though Masonry explicitly rejects any claim to being a religion.*

"My new-cut Ashlar"

(Envoi to Life's Handicap, 1891)

My new-cut ashlar takes the light
 Where crimson-blank the windows flare;
By my own work, before the night,
 Great Overseer I make my prayer.

If there be good in that I wrought,
 Thy hand compelled it, Master, Thine;
Where I have failed to meet Thy thought
 I know, through Thee, the blame was mine.

One instant's toil to Thee denied
 Stands all Eternity's offence,
Of that I did with Thee to guide
 To Thee, through Thee, be excellence.

The depth and dream of my desire,
 The bitter paths wherein I stray,
Thou knowest Who hast made the Fire,
 Thou knowest Who hast made the Clay.

Who, lest all thought of Eden fade,
 Bring'st Eden to the craftsman's brain -
Godlike to muse o'er his own Trade
 And manlike stand with God again.

One stone the more swings into place
 In that dread Temple of Thy Worth.

---

144   John Davies. *'The Masonic poetry of Rudyard Kipling'*, 2006.

It is enough that through Thy grace
 I saw naught common on Thy Earth.

Take not that vision from my ken -
 Oh whatsoe'er may spoil or speed,
Help me to need no aid from men
 That I may help such men as need!

Kipling had a lot of time for Buddhism, with its rejection of dogma in favour of dharma. Buddha at Kamakura *bears comparison with the attitude of respectful doubt in Philip Larkin's* Churchgoing, *though, of course, in an entirely different religious context.*

Buddha at Kamakura

1892

"And there is a Japanese idol at Kamakura"

O ye who tread the Narrow Way
By Tophet-flare to judgment Day,
Be gentle when "the heathen" pray
    To Buddha at Kamakura!

To him the Way, the Law, apart,
Whom Maya held beneath her heart,
Ananda's Lord, the Bodhisat,
    The Buddha of Kamakura.

For though he neither burns nor sees,
Nor hears ye thank your Deities,
Ye have not sinned with such as these,
    His children at Kamakura,

Yet spare us still the Western joke
When joss-sticks turn to scented smoke
The little sins of little folk
    That worship at Kamakura -

The grey-robed, gay-sashed butterflies
That flit beneath the Master's eyes.
He is beyond the Mysteries
    But loves them at Kamakura.

And whoso will, from Pride released,
Contemning neither creed nor priest,
May feel the Soul of all the East
      About him at Kamakura.

Yea, every tale Ananda heard,
Of birth as fish or beast or bird,
While yet in lives the Master stirred,
      The warm wind brings Kamakura.

Till drowsy eyelids seem to see
A-flower 'neath her golden *htee*
The Shwe-Dagon flare easterly
      From Burmah to Kamakura,

And down the loaded air there comes
The thunder of Tibetan drums,
And droned - *"Om mane padme hum's"* -
      A world's-width from Kamakura.

Yet Brahmans rule Benares still,
Buddh-Gaya's ruins pit the hill,
And beef-fed zealots threaten ill
      To Buddha and Kamakura.

A tourist-show, a legend told,
A rusting bulk of bronze and gold,
So much, and scarce so much, *ye* hold
      The meaning of Kamakura?

But when the morning prayer is prayed,
Think, ere ye pass to strife and trade,
Is God in human image made
      No nearer than Kamakura?

The next poem suggests that, while our religion is determined by our up-bringing our longings are universal.

The Prayer

My brother kneels, so saith Kabir,
To stone and brass in heathen wise,
But in my brother's voice I hear
My own unanswered agonies.
His God is as his fates assign,
His prayer is all the world's - and mine.'

[1901]

A Song to Mithras *is a good example of Kipling's ability to put himself in the minds of others. The poet, Alfred Noyes detected in it 'a note of very deep pathos'.*

Mithras, *of course, was the god of the Roman soldier. The irony of the supposed date is that it was not long before Legio XXX, Ulpia Victrix disappeared from history.*

Kipling placed the 30th legion on the Wall without any good authority. Since the poem was written, an inscribed stone was found which seemed to confirm their presence, though some consider it to be a hoax.

'A Song to Mithras'

(Hymn of the XXX Legion: *Circa* A.D. 350)

Mithras, God of the Morning, our trumpets waken the Wall!
'Rome is above the Nations, but Thou art over all!'
Now as the names are answered, and the guards are marched away,
Mithras, also a soldier, give us strength for the day!

Mithras, God of the Noontide, the heather swims in the heat,
Our helmets scorch our foreheads ; our sandals burn our feet.
Now in the ungirt hour; now ere we blink and drowse,
Mithras, also a soldier, keep us true to our vows !

Mithras, God of the Sunset, low on the Western main,
Thou descending immortal, immortal to rise again!
Now when the watch is ended, now when the wine is drawn,
Mithras, also a soldier, keep us pure till the dawn!

Mithras, God of the Midnight, here where the great bull dies,
Look on Thy children in darkness. Oh take our sacrifice !
Many roads Thou hast fashioned: all of them lead to the Light,
Mithras, also a soldier, teach us to die aright!

[1906]

Cold Iron *tells the story of a baron who rebels unsuccessfully against his king but is offered forgiveness. He spurns the king's mercy until the latter reveals himself as Christ.*

On the surface the poem may be seen as an affirmation of Christian faith, with the iron of war being contrasted with the nails of Calvary, but the editor prefers to see it as the poet's faith in the redemptive power of suffering.

Cold Iron

Gold is for the mistress - silver for the maid!
Copper for the craftsman cunning at his trade.
"Good!" said the Baron, sitting in his hall,
"But Iron - Cold Iron - is master of them all!"

So he made rebellion 'gainst the King his liege,
Camped before his citadel and summoned it to siege -
Nay!' said the cannoneer on the castle wall,
But Iron - Cold Iron - shall be master of you all!'

Woe for the Baron and his knights so strong,
When the cruel cannon-balls laid 'em all along!
He was taken prisoner, he was cast in thrall,
And Iron - Cold Iron - was master of it all!

Yet his King spake kindly (Oh, how kind a Lord!):
"What if I release thee now and give thee back thy sword?"
"Nay!" said the Baron, mock not at my fall,
For Iron - Cold Iron - is master of men all."

"Tears are for the craven, prayers are for the clown -
Halters for the silly neck that cannot keep a crown."
"As my loss is grievous, so my hope is small,
For Iron - Cold Iron - must be master of men all!"

Yet his King made answer (few such Kings there be!):
'Here is Bread and here is Wine - sit and sup with me.
Eat and drink in Mary's Name, the whiles I do recall
How Iron - Cold Iron - can be master of men all!'

He took the Wine and blessed It; He blessed and brake the Bread.
With His own Hands He served Them, and presently He said:
"Look! These Hands they pierced with nails outside my city wall
Show Iron - Cold Iron - to be master of men all!

"Wounds are for the desperate, blows are for the strong -
Balm and oil for weary hearts all cut and bruised with wrong.
I forgive thy treason - I redeem thy fall -
For Iron - Cold Iron - must be master of men all!"

"*Crowns are for the valiant - sceptres for the bold!*
Thrones and powers for mighty men who dare to take and hold."
'Nay!' said the Baron, kneeling in his hall,
"But Iron - Cold Iron - is master of men all!
Iron, out of Calvary, is master of men all!"

[1909]

In The Rabbi's Song *Kipling took as his text the words of the book of Samuel: 'For we must needs die, and are as water spilt on the ground, which cannot be gathered up again; neither doth God respect any person. Yet doth he devise means, that His banished be not expelled from Him.' It is the second sentence that is reinforced in the last stanza of this poem.*

The poem achieved rabbinical authority when it was printed in Joseph Friedlander's Standard Book of Jewish Verse.

The Rabbi's Song

(2 Samuel XIV, 14.)

If Thought can reach to Heaven,
 On Heaven let it dwell,
For fear the Thought be given
 Like power to reach to Hell.
For fear the desolation
 And darkness of thy mind
Perplex an habitation
 Which thou hast left behind.

Let nothing linger after -
 No whimpering ghost remain,
In wall, or beam, or rafter,
 Of any hate or pain.
Cleanse and call home thy spirit,
 Deny her leave to cast,
On aught thy heirs inherit,
 The shadow of her past.

For think, in all thy sadness,
 What road our griefs may take;
Whose brain reflect our madness,
 Or whom our terrors shake:

For think, lest any languish
        By cause of thy distress -
The arrows of our anguish
        Fly farther than we guess.

Our lives, our tears, as water,
        Are spilled upon the ground;
God giveth no man quarter,
        Yet God a means hath found,
Though Faith and Hope have vanished,
        And even Love grows dim -
A means whereby His banished
        Be not expelled from Him!

[1909]

Eddi's Service *is a simple poem written to accompany Kipling's short story,* The Conversion of St Wilfred. (Rewards and Fairies). *For an unbeliever like the present editor, it is surprisingly moving. And he can't explain why.*

Eddius Stephanus was chaplain to and biographer of St. Wilfrid, a Benedictine bishop to the South Saxons.

Eddi's Service

(AD 687)

Eddi, priest of St. Wilfred
        In his chapel at Manhood End,
Ordered a midnight service
        For such as cared to attend.

But the Saxons were keeping Christmas,
        And the night was stormy as well.
Nobody came to service,
        Though Eddi rang the bell.

'Wicked weather for walking,'
        Said Eddi of Manhood End.
'But I must go on with the service
        For such as care to attend.'

The altar-lamps were lighted, –
        An old marsh-donkey came,
Bold as a guest invited,
        And stared at the guttering flame.

The storm beat on at the windows,
        The water splashed on the floor,
And a wet, yoke-weary bullock
        Pushed in through the open door.

'How do I know what is greatest,
        How do I know what is least?
That is My Father's business,'
        Said Eddi, Wilfrid's priest.

'But – three are gathered together –
        Listen to me and attend.
I bring good news, my brethren!'
        Said Eddi of Manhood End.

And he told the Ox of a Manger
        And a Stall in Bethlehem,
And he spoke to the Ass of a Rider,
        That rode to Jerusalem.

They steamed and dripped in the chancel,
        They listened and never stirred,
While, just as though they were Bishops,
        Eddi preached them The Word,

Till the gale blew off on the marshes
        And the windows showed the day,
And the Ox and the Ass together
        Wheeled and clattered away.

And when the Saxons mocked him,
        Said Eddi of Manhood End,
'I dare not shut His chapel
        On such as care to attend.'

[1910]

The next poem is a loose translation of an Horatian Ode (Book III, Ode 13), which honoured the spring of Bandusia. It asserts that there is a power that can survive the making and breaking of kingdoms.

The penultimate line has a particular force.

['A Singer spoke to a wayside well']

A Singer spoke to a wayside well
    Or ever Our Lord was born.
And the Powers and Kingdoms rose and fell
    But never a word of the Singer's spell
Was lost, or altered or worn
    Through the thousand years, and the thousand years
Since the drip of the water pleased his ears
    (Oh the Makings and the Breakings, and the Glories and the Fears!)
Or ever Our Lord was born.

[1910]

In this 'cheerfully serious' poem, as Miss Tompkins described it, a 'pilgrim' rejects the need for any intermediary between God and man.

A Pilgrim's Way

I do not look for holy saints to guide me on my way,
Or male and female devilkins to lead my feet astray.
If these are added, I rejoice - if not, I shall not mind,
So long as I have leave and choice to meet my fellow-kind.
      For as we come and as we go (and deadly-soon go we!)
      The people, Lord, Thy people, are good enough for me!

Thus I will honour pious men whose virtue shines so bright
(Though none are more amazed than I when I by chance do right),
And I will pity foolish men for woe their sins have bred
(Though ninety-nine per cent. of mine I brought on my own head).
      And, Amorite or Eremite, or General Averagee,
      The people, Lord, Thy people, are good enough for me!

And when they bore me overmuch, I will not shake mine ears,
Recalling many thousand such whom I have bored to tears.
And when they labour to impress, I will not doubt nor scoff;
Since I myself have done no less and - sometimes pulled it off.
      Yea, as we are and we are not, and we pretend to be,
      The people, Lord, Thy people, are good enough for me!

And when they work me random wrong, as oftentimes hath been,
I will not cherish hate too long (my hands are none too clean).
And when they do me random good I will not feign surprise.
No more than those whom I have cheered with wayside charities.
      But, as we give and as we take - whate'er our takings be -
      The people, Lord, Thy people, are good enough for me!

But when I meet with frantic folk who sinfully declare
There is no pardon for their sin, the same I will not spare
Till I have proved that Heaven and Hell which in our hearts we have
Show nothing irredeemable on either side the grave.
> For as we live and as we die - if utter Death there be -
> The people, Lord, Thy people, are good enough for me!

Deliver me from every pride - the Middle, High, and Low -
That bars me from a brother's side, whatever pride he show.
And purge me from all heresies of thought and speech and pen
That bid me judge him otherwise than I am judged. *Amen*!
> That I may sing of Crowd or King or road-borne company,
> That I may labour in my day, vocation and degree,
> To prove the same in deed and name, and hold unshakenly
> (Where'er I go, whate'er I know, whoe'er my neighbour be)
> This single faith in Life and Death and to Eternity:
> "The people, Lord, Thy people, are good enough for me!"

[1913]

For all that Kipling used the words of a Christian hymn to make a point about human vanity, the title, which comes from Psalm 115, is probably no more than a trope.

"Non Nobis Domine!"

(Written for "The Pageant of Parliament," 1934)

Non nobis Domine!
    Not unto us, O Lord!
The Praise or Glory be
    Of any deed or word;
For in Thy Judgment lies
    To crown or bring to nought
All knowledge or device
    That Man has reached or wrought.

And we confess our blame -
    How all too high we hold
That noise which men call Fame,
    That dross which men call Gold.
For these we undergo
    Our hot and godless days,
But in our hearts we know
    Not unto us the Praise.

O Power by Whom we live -
    Creator, Judge, and Friend,
Upholdingly forgive
    Nor fail us at the end:
But grant us well to see
    In all our piteous ways -
Non nobis Domine! -
    Not unto us the Praise!

MAGIC AND MYSTERY

This section is devoted to poems around the themes of magic and mystery.

The following curious piece appeared as an epigraph to The Children of the Zodiac, *a story which concerns the fear of death. The Kipling Society New Readers' Guide comments that it could, save for its metre, have been written by Ezra Pound.*

['In the hush of an April dawning when the streets were velvety still']

In the hush of an April dawning when the streets were velvety still
The High Gods quitted Olympus and relighted on Ludgate Hill;
The asphodel sprang from the asphalt, the amaranth opened her eyes
And the smoke of the City of London went up to the stainless skies.

"Now whom shall I kiss?" said Venus and "What can I kill?" said Jove,
And "Look at the Bridge", said Vulcan, and "Smut's on my wings", said Love. Then
The High Gods veiled their glories to walk with the children of men.
....
In the hush of an April twilight, to the roar of the Holborn train,
The High Gods sprang from the pavement and went to their place again;
And I heard, tho' none had tolled it, as a great portcullis falls,
In the rear of their wheeling legions, the boom of the bell of St. Paul's.

The Gods in London [1891]

Tomlinson is a lively and imaginative piece about the need to live life to the full and not at second hand. The argument is not entirely persuasive, but the poem contains enough fine imagery to warrant inclusion in this selection.

The Kipling Society New Readers' Guide tells us that 'o'er-sib' is Scottish for 'too closely related'.

Tomlinson

1891

Now Tomlinson gave up the ghost in his house in Berkeley Square,
And a Spirit came to his bedside and gripped him by the hair -
A Spirit gripped him by the hair and carried him far away,
Till he heard as the roar of a rain-fed ford the roar of the Milky Way:
Till he heard the roar of the Milky Way die down and drone and cease,
And they came to the Gate within the Wall where Peter holds the keys.
"Stand up, stand up now, Tomlinson, and answer loud and high
The good that ye did for the sake of men or ever ye came to die -
The good that ye did for the sake of men in little earth so lone!"
And the naked soul of Tomlinson grew white as a rain-washed bone.
"O I have a friend on earth," he said, "that was my priest and guide,
And well would he answer all for me if he were at my side."
- "For that ye strove in neighbour-love it shall be written fair,
But now ye wait at Heaven's Gate and not in Berkeley Square:
Though we called your friend from his bed this night, he could not speak for you,
For the race is run by one and one and never by two and two."
Then Tomlinson looked up and down, and little gain was there,
For the naked stars grinned overhead, and he saw that his soul was bare.
The Wind that blows between the Worlds, it cut him like a knife,
And Tomlinson took up his tale and spoke of his good in life.
"Oh, this I have read in a book," he said, "and that was told to me,
And this I have thought that another man thought of a Prince in Muscovy."
And Peter twirled the jangling Keys in weariness and wrath.

"Ye have read, ye have heard, ye have thought," he said, "and the tale is yet to run:
By the worth of the body that once ye had, give answer - what ha' ye done?"
Then Tomlinson looked back and forth, and little good it bore,
For the Darkness stayed at his shoulder-blade and Heaven's Gate before: -
"Oh, this I have felt, and this I have guessed, and this I have heard men say,
And this they wrote that another man wrote of a carl in Norroway."
"Ye have read, ye have felt, ye have guessed, good lack! Ye have hampered Heaven's Gate;
There's little room between the stars in idleness to prate!
For none may reach by hired speech of neighbour, priest, and kin
Through borrowed deed to God's good meed that lies so fair within;
Get hence, get hence to the Lord of Wrong, for doom has yet to run,
And ... the faith that ye share with Berkeley Square uphold you, Tomlinson!"

. . . .

The Spirit gripped him by the hair, and sun by sun they fell
Till they came to the belt of Naughty Stars that rim the mouth of Hell:
The first are red with pride and wrath, the next are white with pain,
But the third are black with clinkered sin that cannot burn again:
They may hold their path, they may leave their path, with never a soul to mark,
They may burn or freeze, but they must not cease in the Scorn of the Outer Dark.
The Wind that blows between the worlds, it nipped him to the bone,
And he yearned to the flare of Hell-Gate there as the light of his own hearth-stone.
The Devil he sat behind the bars, where the desperate legions drew,
But he caught the hasting Tomlinson and would not let him through.
"Wot ye the price of good pit-coal that I must pay?" said he,
"That ye rank yoursel' so fit for Hell and ask no leave of me?
I am all o'er-sib to Adam's breed that ye should give me scorn,
For I strove with God for your First Father the day that he was born.

Sit down, sit down upon the slag, and answer loud and high
The harm that ye did to the Sons of Men or ever you came to die."
And Tomlinson looked up and up, and saw against the night;
The belly of a tortured star blood-red in Hell-Mouth light;
And Tomlinson looked down and down, and saw beneath his feet
The frontlet of a tortured star milk-white in Hell-Mouth heat.
"O I had a love on Earth," said he, "that kissed me to my fall,
And if ye would call my love to me I know she would answer all."
- "All that ye did in love forbid it shall be written fair,
But now ye wait at Hell-Mouth Gate and not in Berkeley Square:
Though we whistled your love from her bed to-night, I trow she would
not run,
For the sin ye do by two and two ye must pay for one by one!"
The Wind that blows between the worlds, it cut him like a knife,
And Tomlinson took up the tale and spoke of his sin in life:
"Once I ha' laughed at the power of Love and twice at the grip of the
Grave,
And thrice I ha' patted my God on the head that men might call me brave."
The Devil he blew on a brandered soul and set it aside to cool: -
"Do ye think I would waste my good pit-coal on the hide of a brain-sick
fool?
I see no worth in the hobnailed mirth or the jolt-head jest ye did
That I should waken my gentlemen that are sleeping three on a grid."
Then Tomlinson looked back and forth, and there was little grace,
For Hell-Gate filled the houseless Soul with the Fear of Naked Space.
"Nay, this I ha' heard," quo' Tomlinson, "and this was noised abroad,
And this I ha' got from a Belgian book on the word of a dead French lord."
- "Ye ha' heard, ye ha' read, ye ha' got, good lack! and the tale begins afresh
-
Have ye sinned one sin for the pride o' the eye or the sinful lust of the
flesh?"
Then Tomlinson he gripped the bars and yammered, "Let me in -
For I mind that I borrowed my neighbour's wife to sin the deadly sin."
The Devil he grinned behind the bars, and banked the fires high:
"Did ye read of that sin in a book?" said he; and Tomlinson said, "Ay!"

The Devil he blew upon his nails, and the little devils ran,
And he said: "Go husk this whimpering thief that comes in the guise of a man:
Winnow him out 'twixt star and star, and sieve his proper worth:
There's sore decline in Adam's line if this be spawn of earth."
Empusa's crew, so naked-new they may not face the fire,
But weep that they bin too small to sin to the height of their desire,
Over the coal they chased the Soul, and racked it all abroad,
As children rifle a caddis-case or the raven's foolish hoard.
And back they came with the tattered Thing, as children after play,
And they said: "The soul that he got from God he has bartered clean away.
We have threshed a stook of print and book, and winnowed a chattering wind,
And many a soul wherefrom he stole, but his we cannot find:
We have handled him, we have dandled him, we have seared him to the bone,
And sure if tooth and nail show truth he has no soul of his own."
The Devil he bowed his head on his breast and rumbled deep and low:
"I'm all o'er-sib to Adam's breed that I should bid him go.
Yet close we lie, and deep we lie, and if I gave him place,
My gentlemen that are so proud would flout me to my face;
They'd call my house a common stews and me a careless host,
And - I would not anger my gentlemen for the sake of a shiftless ghost."
The Devil he looked at the mangled Soul that prayed to feel the flame,
And he thought of Holy Charity, but he thought of his own good name: -
"Now ye could haste my coal to waste, and sit ye down to fry:
Did ye think of that theft for yourself?" said he; and Tomlinson said, "Ay!"
The Devil he blew an outward breath, for his heart was free from care: -
"Ye have scarce the soul of a louse," he said, "but the roots of sin are there,
And for that sin should ye come in were I the lord alone.
But sinful pride has rule inside – ay, mightier than my own.
Honour and Wit, fore-damned they sit, to each his Priest and Whore:
Nay, scarce I dare myself go there, and you they'd torture sore.
Ye are neither spirit nor spirk," he said; "ye are neither book nor brute -
Go, get ye back to the flesh again for the sake of Man's repute.
I'm all o'er-sib to Adam's breed that I should mock your pain,

But look that ye win to worthier sin ere ye come back again.
Get hence, the hearse is at your door - the grim black stallions wait -
They bear your clay to place to-day. Speed, lest ye come too late!
Go back to Earth with a lip unsealed - go back with an open eye,
And carry my word to the Sons of Men or ever ye come to die:
That the sin they do by two and two they must pay for one by one,
And ... the God that you took from a printed book be with you, Tomlinson!"

People differ about the meaning of the next, haunting poem. To form your own you should read the associated story, The Brushwood Boy.

But you don't need a 'meaning' to drink deep from the poem's images.

The City of Sleep

Over the edge of the purple down,
      Where the single lamplight gleams,
Know ye the road to the Merciful Town
      That is hard by the Sea of Dreams -
Where the poor may lay their wrongs away,
      And the sick may forget to weep?
But we - pity us! Oh, pity us!
      We wakeful; Ah, pity us! -
We must go back with Policeman Day -
      Back from the City of Sleep!

Weary they turn from the scroll and crown,
      Fetter and prayer and plough -
They that go up to the Merciful Town,
      For her gates are closing now.
It is their right in the Baths of Night
      Body and soul to steep,
But we - pity us! ah, pity us!
      We wakeful; Ah, pity us! -
We must go back with Policeman Day -
      Back from the City of Sleep!

Over the edge of the purple down,
      Ere the tender dreams begin,
Look - we may look - at the Merciful Town,
      But we may not enter in!
Outcasts all, from her guarded wall
      Back to our watch we creep:

We - pity us! Ah, pity us!
    We wakeful; ah, pity us! -
We that go back with Policeman Day -
    Back from the City of Sleep!

[1898]

The Runes on Weland's Sword *was written as an epigraph to Kipling's story*, A Centurion of the Thirtieth. As *Peter Keating explained, 'Each stanza represents just one phase of a theme that develops gradually, through all of the stories [in that book], with the recurring unexplained images in the poem representing the 'runes' or inscriptions on the sword.' Its origin notwithstanding, the poem is a satisfying work in its own right, albeit an enigmatic one.*

Runes were the letters of an ancient language. Weland was the legendary Norse blacksmith god.

The Runes on Weland's Sword

(From Puck of Pook's Hill)

1906

A smith makes me
To betray my Man
In my first fight.

To gather Gold
At the world's end
I am sent.

The Gold I gather
Comes into England
Out of deep water.

Like a shining Fish
Then it descends
Into deep Water.

It is not given
For goods or gear
But for The Thing.

The Gold I gather
A King covets
For an ill use.

The Gold I gather
Is drawn up
Out of deep water.

Like a shining Fish
Then it descends
Into deep Water.

It is not given
For gods or gear
But for The Thing.

Under an Act of Charles II's Parliament, the dead were required to be buried in a shroud of English wool. (Nothing theological about this: the measure was simply designed to protect the wool trade.) The next poem tells of a corpse who was not prepared to lie still in her grave.

Old Mother Laidinwool

Enlarged from Old Song

Old Mother Laidinwool had nigh twelve months been dead.
She heard the hops was doing well, an' so popped up her head
For said she: "The lads I've picked with when I was young and fair,
They're bound to be at hopping and I'm bound to meet 'em there!"

> *Let me up and go*
> *Back to the work I know, Lord!*
> *Back to the work I know, Lord!*
> *For it is dark where I lie down, My Lord!*
> *An' it's dark where I lie down!*

Old Mother Laidinwool, she give her bones a shake,
An' trotted down the churchyard-path as fast as she could make.
She met the Parson walking, but she says to him, says she: -
"Oh, don't let no one trouble for a poor old ghost like me!"

'Twas all a warm September an' the hops had flourished grand.
She saw the folks get into 'em with stockin's on their hands -
An' none of 'em was foreigners but all which she had known,
And old Mother Laidinwool she blessed 'em every one.

She saw her daughters picking an' their children them-beside,
An' she moved among the babies an' she stilled 'em when they cried.
She saw their clothes was bought, not begged, an' they was clean an' fat,
An' old Mother Laidinwool she thanked the Lord for that.

Old Mother Laidinwool she waited on all day
Until it come too dark to see an' people went away -

Until it was too dark to see an' lights began to show,
An' old Mother Laidinwool she hadn't where to go.

Old Mother Laidinwool she give her bones a shake
An 'trotted back to churchyard-mould as fast as she could make.
She went where she was bidden to an' there laid down her ghost ...
An' the Lord have mercy on you in the Day you need it most!

> *Let me in again,*
> *Out of the wet an' rain, Lord!*
> *Out of the wet an' rain, Lord!*
> *For it's best as You shall say, My Lord!*
> *An' it's best as You shall say!*

[1906]

285

During and just after terrible wars, the desperate relatives of the dead are understandably tempted by anything, however, bizarre, which promises to offer them access to those they miss.

Kipling wrote the next poem as 'a direct attack at the mania of spiritualism', but he recognized its strong fascination to people like his unstable sister, Trix.

At the request of King Saul the witch of En-dor summoned up the spirit of the dead prophet, Samuel. Annoyed at being disturbed, the witch prophesies the downfall of Saul, which duly happens.

En-Dor

(1914-19-?)

"Behold there is a woman that hath a familiar spirit at En-Dor."

I Samuel, xxviii. 7.

The road to En-dor is easy to tread
    For Mother or yearning Wife.
There, it is sure, we shall meet our Dead
    As they were even in life.
Earth has not dreamed of the blessing in store
For desolate hearts on the road to En-dor.

Whispers shall comfort us out of the dark -
    Hands - ah God! - that we knew!
Visions and voices - look and hark! -
    Shall prove that the tale is true,
And that those who have passed to the further shore
May be hailed - at a price - on the road to En-dor.

But they are so deep in their new eclipse
    Nothing they say can reach,

Unless it be uttered by alien lips
    And framed in a stranger's speech.
The son must send word to the mother that bore,
Through an hireling's mouth. 'Tis the rule of En-dor.

And not for nothing these gifts are shown
    By such as delight our dead.
They must twitch and stiffen and slaver and groan
    Ere the eyes are set in the head,
And the voice from the belly begins. Therefore,
We pay them a wage where they ply at En-dor.

Even so, we have need of faith
    And patience to follow the clue.
Often, at first, what the dear one saith
    Is babble, or jest, or untrue.
(Lying spirits perplex us sore
Till our loves - and their lives - are well-known at En-dor) ...

Oh the road to En-dor is the oldest road
    And the craziest road of all!
Straight it runs to the Witch's abode,
    As it did in the days of Saul,
And nothing has changed of the sorrow in store
For such as go down on the road to En-dor!

[1919]

To his everlasting regret, the present editor has seen the windows of Chartres cathedral only once from the inside, and that on an exceptionally dull day. In default, he has Kipling's sonnet to turn to.

To 'groze' means to trim window glass to shape.

Chartres Windows

1925

Colour fulfils where Music has no power:
By each man's light the unjudging glass betrays
All men's surrender, each man's holiest hour
    And all the lit confusion of our days -
Purfled with iron, traced in dusk and fire,
      Challenging ordered Time who, at the last,
      Shall bring it, grozed and leaded and wedged fast,
      To the cold stone that curbs or crowns desire.
Yet on the pavement that all feet have trod -
      Even as the Spirit, in her deeps and heights,
Turns only, and that voiceless, to her God -
      There falls no tincture from those anguished lights.
And Heaven's one light, behind them, striking through
      Blazons what each man dreamed no other knew.

TEACHER AND PROPHET

Kipling was a prophet, not only in the Biblical sense, but also in the modern sense of a foreteller. It would be fanciful to suggest that he could see into the future, but he certainly saw threats to his country sooner and more clearly than most. Long before the Great War of 1914 he forecast the coming disaster.[145] Decades later, he drew attention to the threat from the Nazis.[146]

Like Churchill, Kipling consistently warned of his country's unpreparedness for war.[147] Like Churchill, his fate was to be proved right.

---

145 'Before a midnight breaks in storm', 1903.

146 *The Islanders*, 1932 (not included), *The Storm Cone*, 1932, and *The Bonfires*, 1933, in which Hitler was represented by Fenris, the world devouring wolf of Nordic legend. In 1934 he wrote of war with Germany, 'Personally, I shall be grateful if we are allowed three years'.

147 *The Islanders*. 1902.

The Dykes was Kipling's *warning of England's lack of preparedness for war. The sentiment was not welcomed by all. He was to return to the same theme a few years later in his more bitter poem,* The City of Brass *(not included here).*

The Dykes

1902

We have no heart for the fishing, - we have no hand for the oar -
All that our fathers taught us of old pleases us now no more;
All that our own hearts bid us believe we doubt where we do not deny -
There is no proof in the bread we eat or rest in the toil we ply.

Look you, our foreshore stretches far through sea-gate, dyke, and groin -
Made land all, that our fathers made, where the flats and the fairway join.
They forced the sea a sea-league back. They died, and their work stood fast.
We were born to peace in the lee of the dykes, but the time of our peace is past.

Far off, the full tide clambers and slips, mouthing and testing all,
Nipping the flanks of the water-gates, baying along the wall;
Turning the shingle, returning the shingle, changing the set of the sand ...
We are too far from the beach, men say, to know how the outworks stand.

So we come down, uneasy, to look, uneasily pacing the beach.
These are the dykes our fathers made: we have never known a breach.
Time and again has the gale blown by and we were not afraid;
Now we come only to look at the dykes - at the dykes our fathers made.

On the marsh where the homesteads cower apart the harried sunlight flies,
Shifts and considers, wanes and recovers, scatters and sickens and dies -
An evil ember bedded in ash - a spark blown west by the wind ...
We are surrendered to night and the sea - the gale and the tide behind!

At the bridge of the lower saltings the cattle gather and blare,
Roused by the feet of running men, dazed by the lantern glare.
Unbar and let them away for their lives - the levels drown as they stand,
Where the flood-wash forces the sluices aback and the ditches deliver inland.

Ninefold deep to the top of the dykes the galloping breakers stride,
And their overcarried spray is a sea - a sea on the landward side.
Coming, like stallions they paw with their hooves, going they snatch with their teeth,
Till the bents and the furze and the sand are dragged out, and the old-time hurdles beneath!

Bid men gather fuel for fire, the tar, the oil and the tow -
Flame we shall need, not smoke, in the dark if the riddled seabanks go.
Bid the ringers watch in the tower (who knows how the dawn shall prove?)
Each with his rope between his feet and the trembling bells above.

Now we can only wait till the day, wait and apportion our shame.
These are the dykes our fathers left, but we would not look to the same.
Time and again were we warned of the dykes, time and again we delayed:
Now, it may fall, we have slain our sons, as our fathers we have betrayed.
....

Walking along the wreck of the dykes, watching the work of the seas!
These were the dykes our fathers made to our great profit and ease.
But the peace is gone and the profit is gone, with the old sure days withdrawn ...
That our own houses show as strange when we come back in the dawn!

David Gilmour described The Islanders *as 'the sternest of all the sermons, the most scolding, intemperate and brilliant of all the prophet's rebukes'. In it, wrote Angus Wilson, '[Kipling] takes each sacred cow of the clubs and the senior common rooms and slaughters it messily before its worshippers' eyes.'*

This furiously bitter poem met with wide resentment when it was first published. Nevertheless, the author followed it up with the equally scathing The Old Guard *(not included here), which condemned the self-serving nature of the officer class.*

The Islanders

1902

No doubt but ye are the People - your throne is above the King's.
Whoso speaks in your presence must say acceptable things:
Bowing the head in worship, bending the knee in fear -
Bringing the word well smoothen - such as a King should hear.

Fenced by your careful fathers, ringed by your leaden seas,
Long did ye wake in quiet and long lie down at ease;
Till ye said of Strife, "What is it?" of the Sword, "It is far from our ken";
Till ye made a sport of your shrunken hosts and a toy of your arméd men.
Ye stopped your ears to the warning - ye would neither look nor heed -
Ye set your leisure before their toil and your lusts above their need.
Because of your witless learning and your beasts of warren and chase,
Ye grudged your sons to their service and your fields for their camping-place.
Ye forced them to glean in the highways the straw for the bricks they brought;
Ye forced them follow in byways the craft that ye never taught.
Ye hindered and hampered and crippled; ye thrust out of sight and away
Those that would serve you for honour and those that served you for pay.
Then were the judgments loosened; then was your shame revealed,
At the hands of a little people, few but apt in the field.
Yet ye were saved by a remnant (and your land's long-suffering star),

When your strong men cheered in their millions while your striplings
went to the war.
Sons of the sheltered city - unmade, unhandled, unmeet -
Ye pushed them raw to the battle as ye picked them raw from the street.
And what did ye look they should compass? Warcraft learned in a breath,
Knowledge unto occasion at the first far view of Death?
So? And ye train your horses and the dogs ye feed and prize?
How are the beasts more worthy than the souls, your sacrifice?
But ye said, "Their valour shall show them"; but ye said, "The end is close."
And ye sent them comfits and pictures to help them harry your foes:
And ye vaunted your fathomless power, and ye flaunted your iron pride,
Ere - ye fawned on the Younger Nations for the men who could shoot and
ride!
Then ye returned to your trinkets; then ye contented your souls
With the flannelled fools at the wicket or the muddied oafs at the goals.
Given to strong delusion, wholly believing a lie,
Ye saw that the land lay fenceless, and ye let the months go by
Waiting some easy wonder, hoping some saving sign -
Idle - openly idle - in the lee of the forespent Line.
Idle - except for your boasting - and what is your boasting worth
If ye grudge a year of service to the lordliest life on earth?
Ancient, effortless, ordered, cycle on cycle set,
Life so long untroubled, that ye who inherit forget
It was not made with the mountains, it is not one with the deep.
Men, not gods, devised it. Men, not gods, must keep.
Men, not children, servants, or kinsfolk called from afar,
But each man born in the Island broke to the matter of war.
Soberly and by custom taken and trained for the same,
Each man born in the Island entered at youth to the game -
As it were almost cricket, not to be mastered in haste,
But after trial and labour, by temperance, living chaste.
As it were almost cricket - as it were even your play,
Weighed and pondered and worshipped, and practised day by day.
So ye shall bide sure-guarded when the restless lightnings wake
In the womb of the blotting war-cloud, and the pallid nations quake.
So, at the haggard trumpets, instant your soul shall leap
Forthright, accoutred, accepting - alert from the wells of sleep.

So at the threat ye shall summon - so at the need ye shall send
Men, not children or servants, tempered and taught to the end;
Cleansed of servile panic, slow to dread or despise,
Humble because of knowledge, mighty by sacrifice.
But ye say, "It will mar our comfort." Ye say, "It will minish our trade."
Do ye wait for the spattered shrapnel ere ye learn how a gun is laid?
For the low, red glare to southward when the raided coast-towns burn?
      (Light ye shall have on that lesson, but little time to learn.)
      Will ye pitch some white pavilion, and lustily even the odds,
      With nets and hoops and mallets, with rackets and bats and rods?
Will the rabbit war with your foemen - the red deer horn them for hire?
Your kept cock - pheasant keep you? - he is master of many a shire.
Arid, aloof, incurious, unthinking, unthanking, gelt,
Will ye loose your schools to flout them till their brow-beat columns melt?
Will ye pray them or preach them, or print them, or ballot them back from your shore?
Will your workmen issue a mandate to bid them strike no more?
Will ye rise and dethrone your rulers? (Because ye were idle both?
Pride by Insolence chastened? Indolence purged by Sloth?)
No doubt but ye are the People; who shall make you afraid?
Also your gods are many; no doubt but your gods shall aid.
Idols of greasy altars built for the body's ease;
Proud little brazen Baals and talking fetishes;
Teraphs of sept and party and wise wood-pavement gods -
These shall come down to the battle and snatch you from under the rods?
From the gusty, flickering gun-roll with viewless salvoes rent,
And the pitted hail of the bullets that tell not whence they were sent.
When ye are ringed as with iron, when ye are scourged as with whips,
When the meat is yet in your belly, and the boast is yet on your lips;
When ye go forth at morning and the noon beholds you broke,
Ere ye lie down at even, your remnant, under the yoke?

No doubt but ye are the People - absolute, strong, and wise;
Whatever your heart has desired ye have not withheld from your eyes.
On your own heads, in your own hands, the sin and the saving lies!

Kipling's great hymn, Recessional does not appear in this anthology for the reasons given in the Preface. Nine years after it was published the poet returned to its theme of the impermanence of earthly pomp and power in this more subdued but no less successful piece.

"Cities and Thrones and Powers"

Cities and Thrones and Powers
 Stand in Time's eye,
Almost as long as flowers,
 Which daily die:
But, as new buds put forth
 To glad new men,
Out of the spent and unconsidered Earth,
 The Cities rise again.

This season's Daffodil,
 She never hears,
What change, what chance, what chill,
 Cut down last year's;
But with bold countenance,
 And knowledge small,
Esteems her seven days' continuance
 To be perpetual.

So Time that is o'er-kind
 To all that be,
Ordains us e'en as blind,
 As bold as she:
That in our very death,
 And burial sure,
Shadow to shadow, well persuaded, saith,
 "See how our works endure!"

[1906]

The Dutch in the Medway *was first published in Kipling and Fletcher's* A School History of England. *It is yet another example of the poet's use of historical example to warn against the dismantling of England's defences.*

Will we ever learn?

The Dutch in the Medway

(1664-1672)

If wars were won by feasting,
    Or victory by song,
Or safety found in sleeping sound,
    How England would be strong!
But honour and dominion
    Are not maintained so.
They're only got by sword and shot,
    And this the Dutchmen know!

The moneys that should feed us
    You spend on your delight,
How can you then have sailor-men
    To aid you in your fight?
Our fish and cheese are rotten,
    Which makes the scurvy grow -
We cannot serve you if we starve,
    And this the Dutchmen know!

Our ships in every harbour
    Be neither whole nor sound,
And, when we seek to mend a leak,
    No oakum can be found;
Or, if it is, the caulkers,
    And carpenters also,
For lack of pay have gone away,
    And this the Dutchmen know!

Mere powder, guns, and bullets,
        We scarce can get at all;
Their price was spent in merriment
        And revel at Whitehall,
While we in tattered doublets
        From ship to ship must row,
Beseeching friends for odds and ends -
        And this the Dutchmen know!

No King will heed our warnings,
        No Court will pay our claims -
Our King and Court for their disport
        Do sell the very Thames!
For, now De Ruyter's topsails
        Off naked Chatham show,
We dare not meet him with our fleet -
        And this the Dutchmen know!

[1911]

Kipling was fond of the dawn and used it as a metaphor often. The Dawn Wind *is his brilliant metaphor for the Renaissance, arguably civilisation's single most important advance. The last line seems to express the poet's mistrust of the clergy.*

The Dawn Wind

(The fifteenth century)

At two o'clock in the morning, if you open your window and listen,
      You will hear the feet of the Wind that is going to call the sun.
And the trees in the shadow rustle and the trees in the moonlight glisten,
      And though it is deep, dark night, you feel that the night is done.

So do the cows in the field. They graze for an hour and lie down,
      Dozing and chewing the cud; or a bird in the ivy wakes,
Chirrups one note and is still, and the restless Wind strays on,
      Fidgeting far down the road, till, softly, the darkness breaks.

Back comes the Wind full strength with a blow like an angel's wing,
      Gentle but waking the world, as he shouts: "The Sun! The Sun!"
And the light floods over the fields and the birds begin to sing,
      And the Wind dies down in the grass. It is day and his work is done.

So when the world is asleep, and there seems no hope of her waking
      Out of some long, bad dream that makes her mutter and moan,
Suddenly, all men arise to the noise of fetters breaking,
      And every one smiles at his neighbour and tells him his soul is his own!

[1911]

*The next, bitterly satirical, poem was provoked by the shady financial deal-
ings of the Liberal Attorney General, Rufus Isaacs concerning a contract for
the setting up of an 'imperial wireless chain' across the world. When shares
in the company rose dramatically, whispers went round that the contract
had been secured with the help of Godfrey Isaacs, the company's manag-
ing director and Rufus' younger brother. Even his explanation to the House
turned out to be a prevarication.*

*Isaacs was later appointed Lord Chief Justice with the title Lord Reading
and went on to become successively Governor General of India and Foreign
Secretary.*

*The Gehazi of the title was Elisha's servant. His name meant 'valley of
deception'.[148]*

Gehazi

1915

Whence comest thou, Gehazi,
        So reverend to behold,
In scarlet and in ermines
        And chain of England's gold ?"
"From following after Naaman
        To tell him all is well,
Whereby my zeal hath made me
        A Judge in Israel."

Well done; well done, Gehazi!
        Stretch forth thy ready hand,
Thou barely 'scaped from judgment,
        Take oath to judge the land
Unswayed by gift of money
        Or privy bribe, more base,

---

148   II Kings, chapters 4 and 5.

Of knowledge which is profit
    In any market-place.

Search out and probe, Gehazi,
    As thou of all canst try,
The truthful, well-weighed answer
    That tells the blacker lie -
The loud, uneasy virtue
    The anger feigned at will,
To overbear a witness
    And make the Court keep still.

Take order now, Gehazi,
    That no man talk aside
In secret with his judges
    The while his case is tried.
Lest he should show them - reason
    To keep a matter hid,
And subtly lead the questions
    Away from what he did.

Thou mirror of uprightness,
    What ails thee at thy vows ?
What means the risen whiteness
    Of the skin between thy brows ?
The boils that shine and burrow,
    The sores that slough and bleed -
The leprosy of Naaman
    On thee and all thy seed ?
        Stand up, stand up, Gehazi,
            Draw close thy robe and go,
      Gehazi, Judge in Israel,
           A leper white as snow !

Kipling was a life-long admirer of the seventeenth century preacher, John Bunyan, author of The Pilgrim's Progress. *Less well known is another of the preacher's work,* The Holy War, *which in this poem Kipling treats as a metaphor for the Great War of 1914-18.*

The Holy War

1917

"For here lay the excellent wisdom of him that built Mansoul, that the walls could never be broken down nor hurt by the most mighty adverse potentate unless the townsmen gave consent thereto." Bunyan's *Holy War.*

A tinker out of Bedford,
    A vagrant oft in quod,
A private under Fairfax,
    A minister of God-
Two hundred years and thirty
    Ere Armageddon came
His single hand portrayed it,
    And Bunyan was his name!

He mapped for those who follow,
    The world in which we are-
"This famous town of Mansoul"
    That takes the Holy War.
Her true and traitor people,
    The Gates along her wall,
From Eye Gate unto Feel Gate,
    John Bunyan showed them all.

All enemy divisions,
    Recruits of every class,
And highly-screened positions
    For flame or poison-gas;

The craft that we call modern,
    The crimes that we call new,
John Bunyan had 'em typed and filed
    In Sixteen Eighty-two.

Likewise the Lords of Looseness
    That hamper faith and works,
The Perseverance-Doubters,
    And Present-Comfort shirks,
With brittle intellectuals
    Who crack beneath a strain -
John Bunyan met that helpful set
    In Charles the Second's reign.

Emmanuel's vanguard dying
    For right and not for rights,
My Lord Apollyon lying
    To the State-kept Stockholmites,
The Pope, the swithering Neutrals
    The Kaiser and his Gott -
Their roles, their goals, their naked souls -
    He knew and drew the lot.

Now he hath left his quarters,
    In Bunhill Fields to lie,
The wisdom that he taught us
    Is proven prophecy -
One watchword through our Armies,
    One answer from our Lands:-
"No dealings with Diabolus
    As long as Mansoul stands!"

A pedlar from a hovel,
    The lowest of the low -
The Father of the Novel,
    Salvation's first Defoe -

Eight blinded generations
Ere Armageddon came,
He showed us how to meet it,
And Bunyan was his name!

Written just before the Great War, the next poem stoically contemplates the carnage ahead as a consequence which, however obscene, mankind cannot escape.

Rebirth

(1914-18)

The Edge of the Evening

If any God should say,
    "I will restore
The world her yesterday
    Whole as before
My Judgment blasted it" - who would not lift
Heart, eye, and hand in passion o'er the gift?

If any God should will
    To wipe from mind
The memory of this ill
    Which is mankind
In soul and substance now - who would not bless
Even to tears His loving-tenderness?

If any God should give
    Us leave to fly
These present deaths we live,
    And safely die
In those lost lives we lived ere we were born -
What man but would not laugh the excuse to scorn?

For we are what we are -
    So broke to blood
And the strict works of war -
    So long subdued
To sacrifice, that threadbare Death commands
Hardly observance at our busier hands.

Yet we were what we were,
       And, fashioned so,
It pleases us to stare
       At the far show
Of unbelievable years and shapes that flit,
In our own likeness, on the edge of it.

[1917]

Dayspring Mishandled *is one of Kipling's most admired short stories. A complex, multi-layered tale of revenge, it is centred upon the following 'forged' 'Chaucerian' poem. In the story revenge is finally abandoned out of compassion for the dying victim.*

'Dayspring' is an old word for dawn. See, for example, Job 32.12, K.J.V.

Gertrude's Prayer

(Modernised from the "Chaucer" of Manallace)

Dayspring mishandled

That which is marred at birth Time shall not mend,
      Nor water out of bitter well make clean;
All evil thing returneth at the end,
      Or elseway walketh in our blood unseen.
Whereby the more is sorrow in certaine -
Dayspring mishandled cometh not againe.

To-bruizéd be that slender, sterting spray
      Out of the oake's rind that should betide
A branch of girt and goodliness, straightway
      Her spring is turnèd on herself, and wried
And knotted like some gall or veiney wen -
Dayspring mishandled cometh not agen.

Noontide repayeth never morning-bliss -
      Sith noon to morn is incomparable;
And, so it be our dawning goeth amiss,
      None other after-hour serveth well.
Ah! Jesu-Moder, pitie my oe paine -
Dayspring mishandled cometh not againe!

[1932]

Fourteen years after the ending of hostilities in what was then the most devastating war in history, Britain's complacent politicians disarmed and stood down the army and navy out of misplaced confidence in their country's freedom from threat. The Storm Cone (a device which signals the coming of high winds) was Kipling's response. He left the menace unspecified, but most saw it as a reinvigorated and bellicose Germany.[149] Four years after this poem was first published Hitler marched into the Rhineland.

The Storm Cone

1932

This is the midnight - let no star
Delude us - dawn is very far.
This is the tempest long foretold -
Slow to make head but sure to hold.

Stand by! The lull 'twixt blast and blast
Signals the storm is near, not past;
And worse than present jeopardy
May our forlorn to-morrow be.

If we have cleared the expectant reef,
Let no man look for his relief.
Only the darkness hides the shape
Of further peril to escape.

It is decreed that we abide
The weight of gale against the tide
And those huge waves the outer main
Sends in to set us back again.

They fall and whelm. We strain to hear
The pulses of her labouring gear,

---

149   An alternative view is that it was designed to encourage Ramsay MacDonald's government of 1931 that was a break-away from the Labour government.

Till the deep throb beneath us proves,
After each shudder and check, she moves!

She moves, with all save purpose lost,
To make her offing from the coast;
But, till she fetches open sea,
Let no man deem that he is free!

AUTOBIOGRAPHICAL

Like most poets, Kipling poured much of himself into his poetry, but it is notoriously difficult to determine what was autobiographical and what mere role playing.

The Two Sided Man *first appeared as an epigraph to a chapter of Kipling's novel, Kim. In that context the 'two sides' of the narrator's brain plainly referred to the eponymous narrator's Indian and British roots. David Gilmour described them thus: 'One side stayed with him in the office and the club, mocking Indians for their political pretensions and their "orientally unclean ... habits". And the other, intensively receptive to sights, smells and sounds, [who] roamed the bazaars and the native states, absorbing the experience without the need to censure.'*

Charles Carrington took a different view when he quoted a friend as saying that Kipling's mind 'was like the leaves of a book which could be quickly turned to suit the company he was in'. Prof. Dobrée had yet a third take on the 'two sides', suggesting they meant that Kipling 'could always see both sides of a question'; while Philip Mason contrasted the 'conscious performer, or the man in the smoking room, [with] someone who could play with children as a child and who was in mysterious touch with the springs of human emotion.'

Take your pick.

The Two-Sided Man

Much I owe to the Lands that grew -
More to the Lives that fed -
But most to Allah Who gave me two
Separate sides to my head.

Much I reflect on the Good and the True
In the Faiths beneath the sun,
But most upon Allah Who gave me two
Sides to my head, not one.

Wesley's following, Calvin's flock,
White or yellow or bronze,
Shaman, Ju-ju or Angekok,
Minister, Mukamuk, Bonze -

Here is a health, my brothers, to you,
However your prayers are said,
And praised be Allah Who gave me two
Separate sides to my head!

I would go without shirt or shoe,
Friend, tobacco or bread,
Sooner than lose for a minute the two
Separate sides of my head!

[1901]

The Second Voyage is a playful piece which sketches out the joys and problems of middle age. (Kipling was 38 at the time of writing.) It is modelled on Enobarbus' speech in Shakespeare's Anthony and Cleopatra, *Act II, Scene 2.*

The Second Voyage

1903

We've sent our little Cupids all ashore -
      They were frightened, they were tired, they were cold:
Our sails of silk and purple go to store,
      And we've cut away our mast of beaten gold.
                           (Foul weather!)
Oh 'tis hemp and singing pine for to stand against the brine,
      But Love he is our master as of old!

The sea has shorn our galleries away,
      The salt has soiled our gilding past remede;
Our paint is flaked and blistered by the spray,
      Our sides are half a fathom furred in weed.
                           (Foul weather!)
And the Doves of Venus fled and the petrels came instead,
      But Love he was our master at our need!

'Was youth would keep no vigil at the bow,
      'Was pleasure at the helm too drunk to steer -
We've shipped three able quartermasters now.
      Men call them Custom, Reverence, and Fear
                           (Foul weather!)
They are old and scarred and plain, but we'll run no risk again
      From any Port o' Paphos mutineer!

We seek no more the tempest for delight,
      We skirt no more the indraught and the shoal -
We ask no more of any day or night
      Than to come with least adventure to our goal'
                           (Foul weather!)

What we find we needs must brook, but we do not go to look,
    Nor tempt the Lord our God that saved us whole.

Yet, caring so, not overmuch we care
    To brace and trim for every foolish blast -
If the squall be pleased to seep us unaware,
    He may bellow off to leeward like the last.
                        (Foul weather!)
We will blame it on the deep (for the watch must have their sleep),
    And Love can come and wake us when 'tis past.

Oh launch them down with music from the beach,
    Oh warp them out with garlands from the quays -
Most resolute - a damsel unto each -
    New prows that seek the old Hesperides!
                        (Foul weather!)
Though we know their voyage is vain, yet we see our path again
    In the saffroned bridesails scenting all the seas!
                        (Foul weather!)

The following sonnet draws attention to the time when a man has to face up to the ultimate test. As the poet explained, 'Ithuriel was that Archangel whose spear had the magic property of showing everyone exactly and truthfully what he was.'

The Hour of the Angel

"Stalky"

Sooner or late - in earnest or in jest -
    (But the stakes are no jest) Ithuriel's Hour
Will spring on us, for the first time, the test
    Of our sole unbacked competence and power
    Up to the limit of our years and dower
Of judgment - or beyond. But here we have
Prepared long since our garland or our grave.
    For, at that hour, the sum of all our past,
    Act, habit, thought, and passion, shall be cast
    In one addition, be it more or less,
    And as that reading runs so shall we do;
    Meeting, astounded, victory at the last,
    Or, first and last, our own unworthiness.
And none can change us though they die to save!
[1913]

Kipling wrote that he had been taught to 'loathe Horace for two years; to forget him for twenty, and then to love him for the rest of my days and through many sleepless nights.'[150] *He and his friend, Charles Graves wrote a number of mock Horation Odes which they published in 1920 under the title,* Q. Horati Flacci-Carminum Librum Quintum *[or the Fifth Book of Horace]. It was, Kipling wrote, but 'a pale rendering' of his Classics master's style at the U.S.C.*

Pindar, of course, was the Greek lyric poet. The sub-title, 'Regulus' is the name of the story the poem was associated with.

Dobrée suggests convincingly that, at the date it was written, the poet was 'detaching himself from affairs ... his ultimate values are becoming clear – poetry, and submission to what the unfaltering gods require'.

A Translation

(Horace, Bk. V. Ode 3,)

Regulus

There are whose study is of smells,
    And to attentive schools rehearse
How something mixed with something else
    Makes something worse.

Some cultivate in broths impure
    The clients of our body - these,
Increasing without Venus, cure,
    Or cause, disease.

Others the heated wheel extol,
    And all its offspring, whose concern
Is how to make it farthest roll
    And fastest turn.

---

150 *Something of Myself.*

Me, much incurious if the hour
        Present, or to be paid for, brings
Me to Brundusium by the power
        Of wheels or wings;

Me, in whose breast no flame hath burned
        Life-long, save that by Pindar lit,
Such lore leaves cold. I am not turned
        Aside to it

More than when, sunk in thought profound
        Of what the unaltering Gods require,
My steward (friend *but* slave) brings round
        Logs for my fire.

[1917]

It must have pleased Kipling to have been installed Lord Rector of St Andrew's by Earl Haig. He held the appointment for three years from 1922 to 1925.

Miss Tompkins described how 'against all his expectations, [Kipling's] inauguration ... broke up, as he says, the frost at his heart and changed and renewed his spirit.'

A Rector's Memory

(St. Andrews, 1923)[151]

The Gods that are wiser than Learning
  But kinder than Life have made sure
No mortal may boast in the morning
  That even will find him secure.
With naught for fresh faith or new trial,
  With little unsoiled or unsold,
Can the shadow go back on the dial,
  Or a new world be given for the old?
But he knows not what time shall awaken,
  As he knows not what tide shall lay bare,
The heart of a man to be taken -
  Taken and changed unaware.

He shall see as he tenders his vows
  The far, guarded City arise -
The power of the North 'twixt Her brows -
  The steel of the North in her eyes;
The sheer hosts of Heaven above -
  The grey warlock Ocean beside;
And shall feel the full centuries move
  To Her purpose and pride.

---

151 This was the date of Kipling's installation. According to Pinney, the poem was probably written in 1926.

Though a stranger shall he understand,
      As though it were old in his blood,
The lives that caught fire 'neath Her hand -
      The fires that were tamed to Her mood.
And the roar of the wind shall refashion,
      And the wind-driven torches recall,
The passing of Time and the passion
      Of Youth over all!
And, by virtue of magic unspoken
      (What need She should utter Her power?)
The frost at his heart shall be broken
      And his spirit be changed in that hour -
Changed and renewed in that hour!

Kipling fought a lifelong battle against depression, which he called 'the immortal woe of life'. The next poem is based upon a legend concerning a clerk in holy orders by the name of Rahere, who, according to legend, founded St Bartholomew's Hospital from his own purse. To this slender tale, Kipling added a later tradition that Rahere was court jester to King Henry I. Gilbert the physician is not a historical character in this context.

Rahere's tomb may be seen in the Priory Church of St. Bartholomew-the-Great in Smithfield, of which he was the founder and first prior.

The poem is a penetrating study of how, though unable to defeat depression, some people can act nobly despite it. This fine poem also contains a most beautiful cameo of 'Love exceeding'.

Rahere

The Wish House

Rahere, King Henry's jester, feared by all the Norman Lords
For his eye that pierced their bosoms, for his tongue that shamed their swords;
Fed and flattered by the Churchmen - well they knew how deep he stood
In dark Henry's crooked counsels - fell upon an evil mood.

Suddenly, his days before him and behind him seemed to stand
Stripped and barren, fixed and fruitless as those leagues of naked sand
When St. Michael's ebb slinks outward to the bleak horizon-bound,
And the trampling wide-mouthed waters are withdrawn from sight and sound.

Then a Horror of Great Darkness sunk his spirit and anon,
(Who had seen him wince and whiten as he turned to walk alone)
Followed Gilbert the Physician, and muttered in his ear,
"Thou hast it, O my brother?" "Yea, I have it," said Rahere.

"So it comes," said Gilbert smoothly, "man's most immanent distress.

'Tis a humour of the Spirit which abhorreth all excess;
And, whatever breed the surfeit - Wealth, or Wit, or Power, or Fame
(And thou hast each) the Spirit laboureth to expel the same.

"Hence the dulled eye's deep self-loathing - hence the loaded leaden brow;
Hence the burden of Wanhope that aches thy soul and body now.
Ay, the merriest fool must face it, and the wisest Doctor learn;
For it comes - it comes," said Gilbert, "as it passes - to return."

But Rahere was in his torment, and he wandered, dumb and far,
Till he came to reeking Smithfield where the crowded gallows are,
(Followed Gilbert the Physician) and beneath the wry-necked dead,
Sat a leper and his woman, very merry, breaking bread.

He was cloaked from chin to ankle - faceless, fingerless, obscene -
Mere corruption swaddled man-wise, but the woman whole and clean;
And she waited on him crooning, and Rahere beheld the twain,
Each delighting in the other, and he checked and groaned again.

"So it comes, - it comes," said Gilbert, "as it came when Life began.
'Tis a motion of the Spirit that revealeth God to man
In the shape of Love exceeding, which regards not taint or fall,
Since in perfect Love, saith Scripture, can be no excess at all.

"Hence the eye that sees no blemish – hence the hour that holds no shame.
Hence the Soul assured the Essence and the Substance are the same.
Nay, the meanest need not miss it, though the mightier pass it by;
For it comes - it comes," said Gilbert, "and, thou seest, it does not die!"

[1926]

Late Came the God *is best understood when read alongside* The Wish House, *one of* Kipling's finest short stories to which it is the epigraph. Story and poem alike deal with the desire that many of us feel at some time, to take on the suffering of a loved one.

That much admired student of the Raj and Kipling scholar, Philip Mason put it amongst his first choice of all the poet's work.

Supporters of the 'misogynist' slur might care to reflect upon the last line.

"Late Came the God"

The Wish House

Late came the God, having sent his forerunners who were not regarded-
Late, but in wrath;
Saying, "The wrong shall be paid, the contempt be rewarded
On all that she hath."
He poisoned the blade and struck home, the full bosom receiving
The wound and the venom in one, past cure or relieving.

He made treaty with Time to stand still that the grief might be fresh -
Daily renewed and nightly pursued through her soul to her flesh -
Mornings of memory, noontides of agony, midnights unslaked for her,
Till the stones of the streets of her Hells and her Paradise ached for her.

So she lived while her body corrupted upon her.
            And she called on the Night for a sign, and a Sign was allowed,
And she builded an Altar and served by the light of her Vision -
            Alone, without hope of regard or reward, but uncowed,
Resolute, selfless, divine.
            These things she did in Love's honour...
What is a God beside Woman? Dust and derision!

[1926]

Andrew Lycett suggests that the next poem referred to Kipling's own recovery from a near psychotic state, but references in the text suggest a more military reading.

The Mother's Son

Fairy-Kist

I have a dream - a dreadful dream
      A dream that is never done,
I watch a man go out of his mind,
      And he is My Mother's Son.

They pushed him into a Mental Home,
      And that is like the grave:
For they do not let you sleep upstairs,
      And you're not allowed to shave.

And it was not disease or crime
      Which got him landed there,
But because They laid on My Mother's Son
      More than a man could bear.

What with noise, and fear of death,
      Waking, and wounds and cold,
They filled the Cup for My Mother's Son
      Fuller than it could hold.

They broke his body and his mind
      And yet They made him live,
And They asked more of My Mother's Son
      Than any man could give.

For, just because he had not died,
      Nor been discharged nor sick,
They dragged it out with my Mother's Son
      Longer than he could stick ...

And no one knows when he'll get well -
      So, there he'll have to be.
And, 'spite of the beard in the looking-glass,
      I know that man is me!

[1927]

For years, Kipling suffered from abdominal pains. This disturbing poem hints that, for some, there can be terrors worse than the corporeal.

Mr Wilkett was a character in the story.

Hymn to Physical Pain

(Mr C.R. Wilkett's Version)

The Tender Achilles

Dread Mother of forgetfulness
      Who, when Thy reign begins,
Wipest away the Soul's distress
      And memory of her sins.

The trusty Worm that diest not -
      The steadfast Fire also,
By thy contrivance are forgot
      In a completer woe.

Thine are the lidless eyes of night
      That stare upon our tears,
Through certain hours which in our sight
      Exceed a thousand years.

Thine is the thickness of the Dark
      That presses in our pain,
As Thine the Dawn that bids us mark
      Life's grinning face again.

Thine is the weariness outworn
      No promise shall relieve,
That says at eve, "Would God 'twere morn"
      At morn, "Would God 'twere eve!"

And when Thy tender mercies cease
    And life unvexed is due,
Instant upon the false release
    The Worm and Fire renew.

Wherefore we praise Thee in the deep,
    And on our beds we pray
For Thy return, that Thou may'st keep
    The Pains of Hell at bay !

[1932]

AFTERWORD
KIPLING: WHAT REMAINS?

Since Kipling's death, society and its moral code have changed to an extent he could not have dreamed of, and poetic forms have moved on in the way they always do. So what remains of Rudyard Kipling the poet?

If we strip away the weaknesses of the man (which were few) and the faults and foibles of his generation (which were many), we are left with a complex individual determined to use his matchless gifts to give voice to the sufferings of the poor and the downtrodden, to face reality so far as he could understand it, and to ceaselessly probe the terrible mysteries of life.

His remains are fittingly interred beside those of Hardy and Dickens.

B. H.

SELECT BIBLIOGRAPHY

Allen, Charles. *Kipling Sahib. India and the Making of Rudyard Kipling.*

Amis, Kingsley. *Rudyard Kipling and his World.*

Birkenhead, Lord. *Rudyard Kipling.*

Carrington, Charles. *Rudyard Kipling, his Life and Work.*

Dobrée, Bonamy. *Rudyard Kipling. Realist and Fabulist.*

Gilmour, David. *The Long Recessional. The Imperial Life of Rudyard Kipling.*

Keating, Peter. *Kipling the Poet.*

Lycett, Andrew. *Rudyard Kipling.*

Mason, Philip. *Kipling, The Glass, the Shadow and the Fire.*

Page, Norman. *A Kipling Companion.*

Pinney, Thomas. *Rudyard Kipling. Something of Myself and other Autobiographical Writings.*

Ricketts, Harry. *The Unforgiving Minute: A life of Rudyard Kipling.*

Rutherford, Andrew. *Kipling's Mind and Art: Selected Critical Essays.*

Tompkins, J.M.S. *The Art of Rudyard Kipling.*

Wilson, Angus. *The Strange Ride of Rudyard Kipling.*

INDEX OF TITLES

INDEX OF FIRST LINES

27782825R00220

Made in the USA
Charleston, SC
22 March 2014